The
PC NC

Handbook

by

Harshad Kotecha

Third Edition 1997

Computer Step
Southfield Road, Southam
Warwickshire CV33 OFB
England

Tel: 01926 817999
Fax: 01926 817005

http://www.computerstep.com

Printed and bound in the United Kingdom

ISBN 1-874029-62-8

*This book is dedicated to my 4-year-old
daughter, Keshvi*

About the Author/Computer Step

Harshad Kotecha has been in the computer industry since the start of the PC revolution and has seen, first hand, the fast development of this technology. In 1983 he graduated (with Honours) in Computer Studies. Since then, he has worked in the computer industry at various levels: from a programmer to a database designer and also as a corporate sales executive.

In 1991 he started his own computer books publishing company, Computer Step, in partnership with his wife Sevanti (also with extensive computing skills, and a degree in Systems Analysis). *The PC Novice's Handbook* (1st edition) was the first book the company published and it became a bestseller overnight. The rest is history – the company now has over 40 current computer titles (written by the best authors in the field) and has become a leading British computer books publisher, exporting their books around the world. However, after all the success, the company never forgets that this is the book that started it all...

Acknowledgements

The author wishes to thank Sevanti for developing the original concept for this book, Leon Robbins for editing and contributing material for this edition, various computer companies for the information provided (especially Microsoft, Dorling Kindersley, Adobe, Corel Corporation, Sage Group Plc), Sunil Kotecha (no relation – Director of Just RAMS Plc) for advice on types of memory used in PCs, and Aartvark Graphics for the front cover drawing.

Contents

5. The Internet 141

Preface

In the home and in the workplace, Personal Computers are a vital and well-established part of the lives of millions of people around the world. Many of these people may find it surprising, then, to learn that the PC has been around for less than 20 years. In this relatively short time, the PC has increased in power and complexity beyond anyone's wildest dreams. However, despite the phenomenal growth in the popularity of PCs, there are still many people who feel alienated by them.

Hence, we have the modern paradox of a computer age in which substantial numbers of individuals are deprived of the benefits of owning and using a computer.

The purpose of this book is to redress this imbalance in a concise, jargon-free language. You will not need a computer dictionary to understand it. You don't even need a PC initially. In fact, you'll be able to make a wiser purchasing decision about which PC and software to buy once you have read this book.

The PC Novice's Handbook will enable you to talk competently to computer dealers and colleagues at work; and you'll be able to follow the growing number of computer publications.

Whether you want to browse the World-Wide Web, learn how to tame Windows, or upgrade your PC, this book will explain how to do so simply and thoroughly in a single section, while a dedicated book of doorstep-thickness might simply confuse you with a mass of barely useful technical facts.

However, as in the acquisition of any knowledge, some strange, new terms must inevitably be introduced. *The PC Novice's Handbook* aims to make this learning process as painless as possible, explaining every new concept as it is introduced. To help you reinforce this new knowledge, an extensive glossary at the back of the book gives definitions of all of these terms, and of others that you might meet in reading other books, talking to other people about computers, or surfing the Internet.

The PC Novice's Handbook is the best all-in-one guide to everything you need to know to make friends with your PC, learn what it can do, and let it start working for you.

The PC Unravelled

Computers fall into three main categories: mainframes, mini-computers (sometimes called *minis*) and micro-computers (*micros*). Mainframes and mini-computers were used by large organisations well before the first micro came on the scene. They tend to take up a lot more space (usually a large computer room needs to be allocated, together with support staff and operators). However, most of these old, large computers do not offer increased processing power compared to the modern micro-computer.

Micros, or micro-computers, were labelled as such because when they were first built they were not taken seriously – they were thought to be too small to be serious computers. In fact, the early micro-computers were games machines built by computer hobbyists in their garages.

The PC is the most popular family of micro-computers today. PC stands for Personal Computer. Because of its size and price it can be purchased to meet just one person's computing needs. Since 1981, when IBM introduced its own micro-computer, called IBM-PC, the term PC has been used to refer to the IBM PC and all other computers with similar specification. These IBM clones are commonly known as 'IBM PC compatibles'.

An IBM PC compatible machine must be able to run the same programs as the IBM PC. For example, Excel (a well known program for the PC) must work in the same way on the compatible as it will on the IBM PC. Also, peripherals like the printer must be interchangeable with the IBM PC.

A brief history

The first IBM PC was a desktop and based on the 8088 chip. It was a basic PC with two floppy disk drives. Some early PCs had hard disks, and some didn't. PCs that did have hard disks were known as XTs.

Moving upwards, the next PC model used a 80286 chip. The IBM 80286 was first launched in 1984. It was also known as an AT or simply a 286 PC. An AT usually had a hard disk. The basic improvement offered by this model over the XT model was in memory. As a result of more memory with this model and its improved memory management capabilities, the AT, unlike the XT, enabled you to have more than one program in memory. However, they aren't powerful enough for running today's advanced applications.

In 1986, Compaq launched a PC using a more powerful 80386 chip. This model was faster than the AT. The main attraction of the 386 model was that it could carry on with certain background jobs, such as printing, whilst the user was working on the main application. However, it was more expensive than a 286 and needed more memory to cope with the 'multitasking' feature.

To overcome the problem of price, a cheaper version of 80386 chip was introduced, known as 80386SX. The original 80386 model was then re-labelled to 80386DX. The 80386SX PC could process data almost as fast as the original 80386 and cost just a little more than the 80286 model. Internally both the chips were identical. The major difference between the two is realised when transmitting data from one PC to another. The 80386DX can transmit data nearly twice as fast as the 80386SX. The 80386SX PC was more popular than the 80386DX. Nevertheless, the 80386DX PC was still widely used for large applications and when it needed to be connected to a *network*.

IBM lost control of the market they originally established. They did not anticipate that PCs would ever become mass market and so they did not protect the original PC design. As a consequence, other companies were free to clone the IBM PC. Not only that, but because of the open architecture of the PC it was possible for clone manufacturers, like Compaq, to improve and expand the capabilities of the IBM PC. Due to this increased competition prices kept on falling and so the market for PCs really started to grow rapidly. IBM had to do something to regain market share and so it launched the PS/2 *(Personal System/2)* range in 1987. Unlike the original IBM PC most models in the PS/2 range were proprietary and the design was registered by IBM. The PS/2 range was based on different technology from the PC and replaced many chips (bought in from other manufacturers) inside the computer, although the main chip used for the processor was still from the 8088 family. IBM tried to use the PS/2 series to introduce yet another operating system standard, called OS/2.

This was to compete head-on with Microsoft's then Windows version 3.1. OS/2 was in fact an impressive operating system providing true multitasking and other improved facilities over Windows. However, due to lack of application software available to work with this operating system and general user resistance to move away from Windows, OS/2 (and the PS/2 range of computers) never did take off in the way IBM had hoped.

You can not write a book on the history of computers in the UK without covering the Amstrad PC – the PC for the masses. Amstrad became a major player in the computer industry with its PCW in 1985 – a personal computer dedicated to word processing. The first IBM PC clone it introduced was PC1512 in the Autumn of 1986. This was the cheapest PC in the UK and became very popular with small companies and private users. Since then Amstrad tried to go upmarket to be accepted by the larger companies. It introduced various new models, but unfortunately could not replicate the success in the highly competitive corporate market. Amstrad then much later in the nineties bought Viglen, a British company which was successful in selling PCs directly to corporates.

In 1989, Intel introduced 80486 chips for the PC. The 486 model was really designed for the power users. It was two to three times faster than the 386 and used to be much more expensive. However, prices plummeted and for some time the 486 was the best seller.

That was, however, only until November 1993 when the next generation of PCs, based on the Pentium chipset, started to take stride. Intel should logically have called the Pentium processor a 80586, but discovered that they could not patent this number. Initially, only lower end Pentiums were available – 60 Mhz, 75 MHz and 90 MHz. Then came 100, 120, 133, 166 and 200 MHz chips. These were extremely fast compared to the 486 and as they quickly became competitively priced, most manufacturers only supplied Pentium PCs; from low-end Pentiums to 'all-singing-and-dancing' multimedia models.

In November 1995 Intel released a Pentium Pro chip which was faster than the original Pentium. Then, in January 1997, the first Pentium PCs equipped with Intel's new MMX *(MultiMedia eXtensions)* technology started to appear. These are designed to offer much better quality and performance for multimedia systems.

Even to this day the PC market is expanding at a rapid pace as newer, better and more powerful models replace older machines at the same price or lower.

Hardware

Your computer consists of hardware and software. Hardware is the term used to refer to the physical, tangible elements of your computer. These are parts you can see and touch. Software (or programs), on the other hand consists of encoded statements, which instruct the computer to perform the required tasks. A CD-ROM you insert in your PC, for instance, is hardware. The programs on it are collectively termed software. Software is an important part of your computer – without it your computer is simply a mass of electronic components.

The subject of software deserves a whole section of its own. Section 2 is dedicated to cover this topic in detail. The rest of this section looks at PC hardware.

A PC consists of the following basic hardware parts:

- Keyboard
- Monitor
- System unit

Keyboard

The keyboard is an input device that you need to give instructions to your computer. The standard English language keyboard is called a QWERTY because they are the first six letters on the top row. The keys are essentially the same as those found on a typewriter. A computer keyboard, however, will have some additional keys:

Enter

When you type commands from your keyboard, you need to press the Enter key. It is only when you press this key that the computer reads your entry. This key is also used like the 'carriage return' on a typewriter to mark the end of a paragraph.

Control (marked 'Ctrl') and Alternative ('Alt')

These are used with each other or other keys for specific purposes, largely dictated by software. For instance, 'Ctrl', 'Alt', and 'Delete' keys are pressed together to restart, or in computer terminology, reboot your PC.

Function keys

These are labelled F1, F2, F3 and so on until F12. They are used by various software packages to instruct the PC to perform specific tasks. For example, F1 will usually provide instant on-screen help on your software.

Escape (marked Esc)

Again largely controlled by software. It is usually used to go back from a specific screen or option selected from a software application.

Page Up, Page Down, Insert & Delete

These keys are usually used within a word processor. They allow you to page up and down in a long document or edit text using Insert or Delete keys.

Arrow keys

There are four keys near the numeric key-pad on the right; each with an arrow pointing in different directions. These enable you to move the cursor – usually a vertical dash used for positioning within text blocks in various software applications.

Print Screen

Copies an image of your screen onto the Windows clipboard.

There is not much to choose from between different makes of keyboards – a lot depends on your own preferences. Some keyboards have a 'positive feel' which means that they click when you press a key. Others are silent. The best way to choose a keyboard is to try typing on a few. Buy the one that feels right. When you buy a new PC, the keyboard is of course part of it.

The Microsoft Natural Keyboard is, however, a little different. The main keys are split into right and left-hand groups and also sloped to ensure a natural wrist posture. It also includes a couple of additional keys as shortcuts to using Windows.

If the keyboard is the main device for you to talk to your computer, then the monitor is the main device for your computer to talk to you.

Monitor

Monitors are also called screens, VDUs *(Video Display Units)* or just displays. Monitors look just like your portable television sets. In fact, earlier home computers did not come with monitors. Television screens were used instead. This is a cheaper alternative but the display quality is poor compared to the dedicated monitors you can buy as part of your computer today.

A PC monitor is controlled by a *graphics card* (sometimes called a *video card*). This is a circuit board placed inside your computer before the monitor is installed. A graphics card translates data from the computer into signals that can be understood by the monitor. The monitor and the graphics card must be compatible with each other for this to work.

Almost any screen you buy today is likely to be based on SVGA *(Super Video Graphics Array)*. These can provide resolutions of 1280 x 1024 pixels and up to 16 million colours. If you're buying a new monitor/graphics card ensure that it's possible to display at least up to 1,024 x 768 pixels (or dots). At this resolution you'll be able to display the following number of colours depending on the amount of memory available on the card.

Type	Memory	Number of Colours
8-bit	1MB	256
16-bit	2MB	65,000
24-bit	4MB	16,000,000

You'll still be able to display in a lower resolution mode, like for standard VGA at 640 x 480 pixels or at 800 x 600 pixels. In higher resolution modes more of the image will fit on your screen, but it will be smaller.

Therefore it is recommended that for high resolution display you buy a larger size monitor. A standard 14-inch is actually a little small for most needs; you will benefit greatly from an increase of an inch in size. If you need to view images in great detail and clarity, such as for desktop publishing purposes, you will probably find that you need at least a 17-inch monitor. One important thing to keep in mind when considering the sizes of monitors you see advertised is the way in which the manufacturer has measured the size of the screen. All measurements are made diagonally from one corner of the screen to another, but while an advertisement might describe a 15-inch screen, this could actually be the size of the *cathode ray tube* (CRT) – what you actually see, once it is in its casing, could be only 14 inches of screen. A 21-inch screen is superb but you may find that the cost is greater than the rest of your PC system.

Another important factor to consider is the refresh rate of the monitor. This is the number of frames displayed on screen every second. It is measured in Hertz. A minimum rate at a resolution of 1,024 by 768 should be 70Hz. A lower refresh rate will cause flickering and although sometimes it's not bad enough for you to notice it, you'll find it tiring staring at your monitor for long periods.

It's also best to ensure that your monitor is non-interlaced for a flicker-free display. Interlacing does not usually come into play until you display at higher resolutions above 800 x 600 pixels. The way interlaced monitors work is that they only display half the image on each pass of the beam. Say on the first pass odd lines are drawn, then on the second pass the remaining even lines are filled. So even though you have a high resolution monitor it is working at only half the speed. Interlaced monitors are cheaper but try and avoid them.

If you're going to be running a lot of multimedia applications ensure that the card also has VRAM *(Video RAM)* fitted for better performance (see the *RAM* topic later). Also, if you are likely to be playing a lot of the newer 3D games on your PC then get one with a 3D graphics accelerator.

System unit

The system unit is the primary part of your PC. It is a plastic or a metal case containing several important elements that make a computer what it is.

The basic parts that reside within the system unit are as follows:

- Microprocessor
- Memory
- Hard disk drive
- Floppy disk drive
- CD-ROM drive

Microprocessor

A microprocessor is often referred to as the 'brain' of a computer. This is because it is here that all the work is done. The processor *(also called CPU: Central Processing Unit)* obeys software instructions and manipulates relevant data. It has the ultimate control over all other components, such as the memory, hard disk and printer.

A microprocessor is a microchip, similar to those found in washing machines, microwaves and television sets. Most PCs produced today use Intel Corporation's fast Pentium processor, but earlier machines used chips with names like 80386 and 80486.

Memory

Computer memory holds information that is required by the processor. This information may be the data to be processed or the programs to process the data. On the surface, the memory is just another micro-chip. However, what is crucial is what the chip contains. There are two types of memory: *Read Only Memory* (ROM) and *Random Access Memory* (RAM).

ROM

When you switch on your PC you will notice that it takes a few seconds before it allows you to interact with it. During these few seconds the PC is running various routines. These routines, or programs, consist of self tests for the PC to ensure that all its parts are working properly. These programs are held in the ROM. The other software that resides within the ROM are programs to take care of routine jobs such as reading instructions from the keyboard and sending characters to the screen. Everything in the ROM has to be installed when the chip is manufactured and you cannot change or erase its contents. Hence, it is called Read Only Memory.

RAM

When you switch on your PC, RAM is available to store information. Unlike the data held in ROM, the data in RAM can be changed or erased. However, RAM just holds 'live' data consisting of the software you are using plus any data files that you may create or update. When you switch off your PC everything in RAM is wiped off.

There are two basic types of RAMs used in PCs depending on the task: DRAM *(Dynamic RAM)*, and SRAM *(Static RAM)*. DRAM, which is used for the main memory banks of a PC, stores data using millions of tiny capacitors, which, when charged up with an electrical current, maintain that charge for about a thousandth of a second. However, since the capacitors discharge so quickly, those that are meant to be charged need to be constantly recharged in order to preserve their data. The upshot of this is that, since the DRAM circuits are always so busy, whenever some of the data they hold needs to be read or replaced with new data, the access time can be impaired somewhat.

DRAMs can be divided further – for example: EDO RAM *(Extended Data Out RAM)* offers better performance because it can start a new memory access cycle even before the previous one is completed. SDRAM *(Synchronous DRAM)* is the latest type used for standard memory in PCs – it is roughly twice as fast as EDO RAM because it can work at the clock speed of the main processor (CPU). This frees the CPU, providing much better performance than conventional memory devices.

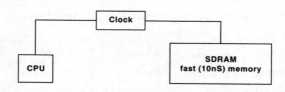

Memory speeds are measured in nanoseconds (nS). One nanosecond is 10^{-9}th (a very small fraction) of a second.

SRAM, on the other hand, stores memory using transistors, which effectively 'lock' in either an 'on' or an 'off' position. This means that the data held by the transistors does not continually need to be refreshed, so the circuit is less busy. When the processor reads from or writes to SRAM, then, it can do so more quickly because little else is going on. Despite its quicker access time, SRAM is not used in all memory circuits: the increased complexity of its design means that it is more costly to manufacture, and that it cannot approach the vast amounts of memory that can be given by DRAM. Therefore, SRAM is usually used for *cache memory*. This can be thought of as a temporary "buffer" between the main RAM and the CPU. When a segment of program is fetched from RAM, a copy is also written to cache memory. When the same segment is required again it is fetched from the cache memory instead of RAM. Since accessing cache memory is much quicker than RAM, the performance of all your applications is improved.

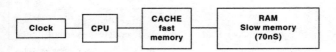

When buying a PC, you should ensure that it has at least 256 Kbytes of *burst mode pipeline cache*.

Hard disk drive

RAM is a temporary storage media. For more permanent storage you need to use disks. These may be floppy disks (covered next) or hard disks. Both are coated with a magnetic film on which data is written. Hard disks, however, contain several magnetically coated platters which are more rigid and spin at much faster speed. There is a read/write head for each surface of the platter controlled by a single positioning mechanism – they float just above the disk without touching (if they touched the surface, your hard disk would wear out in minutes!). The

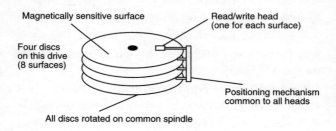

Magnetically sensitive surface

Read/write head
(one for each surface)

Four discs
on this drive
(8 surfaces)

Positioning mechanism
common to all heads

All discs rotated on common spindle

read/write heads detect magnetic fluctuations on the disk surface and that is how information is read; very much like how a head on a tape recorder works. The heads move between concentric circles on each disk platter, called *tracks*. Each track is divided into *sectors* and this is where the data is stored. The whole mechanism is sealed in a robust chamber of aluminium casing rather than the plastic casing used for floppies and then finally incorporated into a *hard disk drive*.

Hard disks can store a lot more data and the processor can access data from a hard disk much faster than from a floppy disk. Hence, the PC can work much faster.

While some of the earlier PCs used a floppy disk drive as their primary means of data storage, all PCs produced nowadays come with a built-in hard disk drive (in addition to a floppy disk drive). The storage capacity of modern hard disks is rarely less than a *gigabyte* (Gb for short), and can run into several gigabytes. A *megabyte* (Mb) is just over a million characters, while a Gb is a thousand megabytes. So a 1Gb hard disk can store over one thousand million characters.

The most common type of hard disk drive used today is EIDE *(Extended Integrated Drive Electronics)* which is the same as the original IDE drive but offers higher storage capacities. Most of the electronics in an EIDE drive are built into the drive itself, so the disk controller is kept very simple. An alternative to EIDE is the SCSI *(Small Computer Systems Interface)* drive. This has the advantage that you can easily attach other hard disk drives and peripherals to the same SCSI controller, thereby freeing the CPU from performing data transfers so that it can get on with other useful work. The disadvantage of a SCSI drive is that it is more expensive, so you should only consider it if you are likely to have many more drives/peripherals attached.

Even though you have a hard disk, you will still need a floppy disk drive, and perhaps also a CD-ROM drive. When you buy software it will come on one or more floppy disks, or, increasingly, on a single CD-ROM. The floppy disk or CD-ROM drive is used to install the software onto hard disk, where it is stored until required. Every time you use the software, it is transferred to the RAM automatically. The processor then addresses this memory to process instructions and data stored here.

Floppy disk drive

Your floppy disk drive, which looks like a hole on the face of your system unit, is used to read floppy disks. In the past, floppy disks for PCs were 5¼ inch or 3½ inch. These measurements denoted the diameters of the disks.

Any new PC you buy nowadays will have a 3½ inch disk drive. These disks have greater storage capacity and are better protected with their hard plastic casing. You can have more than one floppy disk drive in your system, although for most applications a hard disk and one floppy disk drive is quite adequate.

The storage capacity of disks can be measured in *bytes*. One byte is equivalent to one character. A *kilobyte* is 1024 bytes or characters and it is abbreviated as K or Kb. Some early 3½ inch disks could store only 360K or 720K, but nowadays all floppy disks on which you will buy software, or want to store data, will have a capacity of 1.44 Mb. (Mb is a thousand kilobytes or approximately 1 million bytes.) These are double-sided, high density (HD) disks compared to the earlier single density (SD) and double density (DD) disks. You can also purchase higher capacity floppies and drives offering capacities up to 2.8 Mb – these are clasified as extended density disks (or ED). All disks now are double sided.

Floptical disks used with the appropriate drive can offer even higher capacity removable storage medium. These use optical storage technology similar to that used in CD-ROMs to provide that extra storage capacity.

CD-ROM drive

The CDs used by computers are exactly the same as the sort you buy music on: the only difference is the information recorded on them (if you put a CD-ROM in your audio CD player, you'll just hear a lot of whirring and whistling). Unlike your hard drive and floppy drive, which store and read information electromagnetically, CDs work on an optical basis. The surface of a CD is covered with millions of bumps and grooves, used to encode the information stored. In order to read a CD, a

laser beam is pointed onto its surface. The quality of the light that bounces back onto a receptor is used to determine whether the beam was pointing at a bump or a groove, and as the disk is spun around under the laser beam, the encoded data is read and decoded.

When you come to buy a CD-ROM *(Compact Disc Read Only Memory)* drive, either separately or as part of your computer system, the main choice you will have to make is between drives of different speed. The earliest standard type of CD-ROM drive ran at *single-speed*. This was followed by the *double-speed* drive, the *quad-speed*, *six-speed*, *eight-speed* and even *twelve-speed*. Nowadays, you are unlikely to be able to buy anything less than a quad-speed drive; these are sufficiently fast for most applications. Beware, however, of being persuaded by hardware manufacturers and dealers to spend lots of money on the fastest drives available. Surprisingly, an eight-speed drive is unlikely in practice to perform twice as fast as a quad-speed drive. The manufacturers aren't lying: while an eight-speed drive is physically capable of running at twice the speed of a four-speed drive, its performance on an average computer will be impaired because of a lack of processor speed. So while the CD-ROM drive might be ready to supply a piece of information, the processor may not be ready to accept it because it is still dealing with the information that it was supplied with a split-second ago. Thus, the computer will constantly be trying to catch up with the CD-ROM, and the potential improvement in access speed will not be realised. Whereas the early double-speed drives only delivered a data transfer rate of 300Kb/second, a twelve-speed drive today spins six times faster and therefore can potentially offer a transfer rate of 18Mb/second.

Any CD-ROM drive should allow you to play ordinary music CDs in it. Windows comes with an application called *CD Player*, which will allow you to play music in the background while you continue with any other program. You move from one track to another not by using physical buttons on the casing of the CD-ROM drive (it won't have any, except for an eject button), but by clicking with your mouse on buttons in the *CD Player* window. Most CD-ROM drives have an audio socket and volume control somewhere on their surface, enabling you to plug in some headphones, but if you have a sound card you'll probably want to use that to play the music over your external speakers.

Peripherals

We have looked at the basic components of PCs. Some of the other peripheral parts that are added to the PC to make it more useful or easier to use are:

- Mouse
- Printer
- Scanner
- Modem
- Sound card
- CD-R drive
- Backup drive
- Joystick
- Graphics tablet
- Plotter

Mouse

Although a mouse is an optional input device to attach to your computer, it is essential to have one to use today's new windows-based software.

The mouse is placed on your desk, usually on top of a 'mouse mat', next to your keyboard. To move the mouse pointer on your screen, just move your mouse up, down, left or right and then click with the left mouse button when the pointer is in the desired position. Some features in software will be accessible by clicking on the right mouse button – like to display an appropriate shortcut menu to select from depending on where you use it from (context-sensitive).

The Microsoft mouse is one of the most comfortable to use. It is shaped for enhanced hand support. The Microsoft Intellimouse goes even further – it has a little wheel in the middle of the left and right buttons. You can rotate this wheel to scroll through information displayed inside a window or zoom in and out of documents.

Printer

Although the printer is not the main part of your PC, it is very unlikely that you will be able to do without it. Printers allow you to produce "hard copies" of your work. If you are using your PC for writing letters, you will need a printer to produce them on paper. If you are working on business applications such as accounting, you will need to print reports from it at some stage.

There are many choices for printers. The best way to understand the pros and cons is to see how they work.

Dot matrix

These printers are usually low-priced and used widely. The print heads contain either 9 or 24 pins. To print a character, the printer hammers these pins at the ribbon, creating dots on the paper, in the shape of the character. You can easily recognise output from a dot matrix printer – the characters are made of several tiny dots.

The print quality of 24-pin printers is much finer, but 9-pin printers are cheaper. The best quality output you can get from dot matrix printers is called *"near letter quality"* (NLQ); produced by 24-pin printers. The 9-pin printers achieve NLQ by printing repeatedly until the dots are joined-up, but this slows down the speed drastically. And it is the speed that separates low-end models from higher ones. Speed can vary from about 180 characters per second (cps) to over 360 cps.

Dot matrix printers are ideal for printing on continuous stationery. For example, invoices, labels and so on. You can even use multi-part paper. However, they are not recommended for high quality printing.

Ink jet / Bubble jet

These printers work like dot matrix printers, but instead of shooting pins against the ribbon, they shoot a fine jet of ink and therefore do not need ribbons. You can also have different colour inks. These printers are *not* very expensive to buy but they can be quite expensive to run.

The basic technology used in bubble jet printers varies very slightly from ink jet printers. The print heads in bubble jets contain thin nozzles, which hold ink. They also have a heating component. When you start a print job, the heating component produces bubbles that expand and fire the ink at the paper.

Both these types of printers use non-mechanical techniques to print, so they are very quiet. The quality is also pretty good.

If your budget is limited and you need to produce impressive documents (especially if they need to be in colour), ink/bubble jet printers are good alternatives to laser printers. They cost a lot less.

Laser
Laser printers are popular in business today because they produce very impressive documents with graphics.

Although a little more pricey than ink jet printers, they can produce high print quality – almost as good as typesetting. Hence, the term "*near typeset quality*" is used to describe output from laser printers.

These printers use laser technology to create characters and shapes on paper. They work in a similar way to photocopiers, whereby an image is copied a page at a time. Unlike other printers, where a character is processed one at a time, laser printers process a whole page at a time. Therefore the printing speed for laser printers is measured in pages per minute.

As well as the excellent print quality, laser printers are fast and very quiet – and cheap to run. Mono output lasers have really come down in price in the last few years and they now cost just a little more than ink jet printers. However, a colour laser printer is still a lot more expensive than a colour ink jet printer.

Also, a PostScript laser printer will be more expensive than a normal one. PostScript is a page description language which instructs your printer what to print. It is a standard developed by Adobe and used in professional desktop publishing. The main advantage is that it is a piece of software that is device-independent, so your work will look exactly the same on a 75dpi (dots-per-inch) monitor as printed on your own 300dpi laser printer.

If you take the same piece of work to a photosetting bureau to reproduce it on a high resolution (2,400dpi) image-setter, the results will still be the same without the need for re-formatting, although the quality of output will be much finer.

Scanner

A scanner essentially uses the same technology as a fax machine. It reads an image from paper and instead of sending it down the telephone line, converts it to a format that your PC can understand. The computer holds the image as a graphics file, which you can print, amend or add to other documents.

You will need a scanner if you want to include pictures, such as photographs, in your document. For the best resolution, buy a flat-bed scanner. Hand-held ones are

cheaper, but the quality of pictures produced is not as good. Check the resolution of images generated by a scanner before buying it. Most flatbeds have transparency kits for slides or negatives as optional extras.

To scan photographic transparencies to very high professional quality you will need a drum scanner. This is very expensive – probably costing more than your computer; so if you only have an occassional need for one it is far more cost-effective to use a bureau service.

Modem

You will need a modem to use the Internet or any online services offered by CompuServe, America On-Line (AOL), or Microsoft Network (MSN). Let us first look at how a modem works to understand its purpose in computer communications.

A computer can only really differentiate between high voltage and low voltage. After all, it is merely an electronic device. However, for it to be of any use to us, we need the computer to identify letters, numbers and special characters (like %, *). This is achieved by representing high voltage, inside a computer, as '1' and low voltage as '0'. And then, by using a series of '1's and '0's, all the characters on your keyboard are defined inside a PC. This method of representation is called a *Binary system*.

For example, the number '1' is represented by 00000001, number '2' by 00000010, the letter 'A' by

01000001, and so on. Each '0' or a '1' is called a *bit* (short for BInary digiT). A group of 8 bits represents a character or a value and it is called a *byte*.

Since everything inside a computer is represented by a string of '1's and '0's, the computer signal, or output that is generated by a computer, is a square wave:

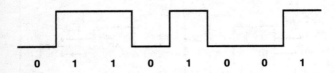

This is in sharp contrast to the type of wave we generate when we speak on the telephone. The human voice will generate a range of frequencies and thus produces a sine wave:

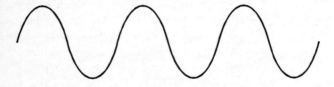

A modem converts computer generated output (a square wave) into frequencies that can be transmitted on a telephone line (a sine wave). This is necessary because the telephone line is not designed ideally to carry computer-generated signals. The receiving computer at the other end also requires a modem to convert back the telephone signals into computer ones. Hence, the name modem is derived from MOdulator-DEModulator.

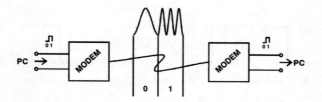

Modems can either be available as a 'box', which you connect to the serial port (one of the sockets at the back of a PC) and the telephone line (called an external modem), an expansion card that you fit inside your computer (internal modem), or a PC card you plug into a notebook. External modems are the most popular because you can *see* various light indicators informing you whether the modem is working, receiving data, etc. Also, it is easier to detach/attach an external modem between PCs.

The speed of data transmission depends directly on the type of modem you use. The reason for this is that the receiving modem must sample the frequency for a certain period of time to determine whether it is receiving a '0' or a '1'. This sampling time determines the transmission speed. Modems that only require a short sampling time and therefore offer faster transmission speeds are usually more expensive. Transmission speeds are measured in *bits per second (bps)* or thousand bits per second (kbps).

Obviously, the faster the transmission speed the cheaper it is going to be in terms of telephone bills, but the initial modem cost is going to be a little higher.

The price of modems has fallen dramatically in the past few years, and today it is not worth buying anything less than a 33.6 kbps modem: it might cost a bit more than a 28.8 kbps modem, but it will pay for itself quickly in the amount you save on your phone bill. Any such modem you buy nowadays will be a "fax modem", which allows you also to use your computer to send and receive faxes as if it were a normal fax machine. Ignore the warnings you read in magazines and books last year about the exorbitant cost of high-speed modems: today you can buy a 33.6 kbps fax modem for under £150.

Sound card

Most programs you buy these days incorporate sound effects that can only be played if you have a sound card to make sense of them – otherwise, you'll only hear a stock bleep from your PC speaker whenever your computer wants to communicate with you audibly. You'll always be able to get along adequately using programs that only use incidental sound effects, but for any true multimedia application, such as Microsoft's *Encarta* encyclopedia (see Section 2 on Software), you'll need a sound card if you don't want to miss out on an integral part of the experience.

A sound card translates between digital data and analogue sound, and works in two ways: you can either use it to play sounds that have already been recorded, via the speakers connected to it; or you can use it to record sounds digitally on your computer, either from a microphone you connect to it or from a direct link to some other audio source. The socket you'll need to use to plug in a microphone can be found at the back of your computer, along with all the other outlets and expansion ports.

You should also find a socket that will enable you to connect the card to a hi-fi amplifier, and one that will enable your computer to communicate with MIDI-compatible equipment. The term MIDI, standing for *Musical Instrument Digital Interface*, refers to the system of conventions established to allow electronic instruments to communicate with each other, and with computers designed to control them. This means that if you have, say, a keyboard with a MIDI interface, then you'll be able to connect it to your MIDI compatible sound card, and use the computer to record data concerning the notes you play. The sounds will be recorded not as digitised recordings of an analogue signal, along with all the accompanying hissing and crackling, but as values describing the notes' pitch, duration, etc., so that they can then be edited easily using the computer alone. You might then use a dedicated program to convert this data into sheet music, for others with more conventional musical instruments to play. One of the most significant applications of MIDI, however, is the potential it allows for using a computer to control the output of an instrument, or a whole group of instruments. When a computer does this, it is acting as a *sequencer*. Let us say that a keyboard and a drum machine were both MIDI-connected to a computer running a sequencer application. The computer could be used to send synchronised signals to both instruments simultaneously, instructing them as to which notes to play, when and for how long to play them, and what voice to play them in.

The MIDI data does not contain specific information (such as the quality of the tone) about what voice to play each individual note in, and so it needs an additional source of information explaining how to synthesise the sound of, say, a violin, and how this is different from that of a drum or a piano. The method used to do this allows us to split sound cards into two groups. Most cards use a simple FM *(Frequency Modulation)* synthesiser chip, which contains fairly rudimentary information about the sounds of a limited number of different instruments. These sounds are determined by setting certain values digitally, and are not based directly on recordings of the sounds of real instruments. Much better quality is achieved by *wavetable* sound cards, which contain a richer digital description of the characteristics of an instrument's tone, recorded from real instruments and stored on a ROM (Read-Only Memory) chip.

Aside from MIDI performance, the quality of a sound card is determined largely by the frequency at which it samples sounds, and by the richness of information incorporated in each split-second sample. Let us say that I wanted to record a one-second sample of my speech as a wave file, so that I could send it to someone else via the Internet, or use it as a sound to be played by Windows when a certain system event occurred. In order to digitise my analogue voice, the sound card would split that second of recording time into a number of minute slices – a typical number would be 16,000, giving a 16KHz sample. For each of these slices in time, the volume, pitch and quality of the sound detected would be recorded.

If, instead, only 8,000 samples were made in that second, the amount of data captured would be half as detailed: minute pieces of information would be missed out. On the other hand, if a 32KHz sample were made, the quality would be much richer.

The other factor, the size of the sample at each of those time-slices, relates to the amount of information that is recorded at each split-second. This is often referred to as the size of the *sample word*. You will see advertisements for sound cards offering 8-bit, 16-bit and 32-bit sample words. A 32-bit sound card is able to differentiate twice as finely between different levels of pitch, volume and tone quality as a 16-bit card, but the resulting file will take up twice as much room.

One of the most popular and long-standing makes of sound card is the Creative Labs SoundBlaster. This has now become the industry standard, and so you should be very wary of buying a sound card that isn't labelled as being "SoundBlaster compatible".

Also check that the sound card is compatible with your CD-ROM drive if you're not buying it together as part of a multimedia system. A 16-bit card capable of 44KHz frequencies should be your minimum requirement.

CD-R drive

CD-ROMs, with their huge storage capacity and current

cheapness, would seem to be the ideal alternative to floppy disks, which, though also cheap, can carry only relatively little data, and are prone to corruption by strong magnetic fields. They do indeed seem to be taking over from floppies in many areas (the installation disks of most large software applications nowadays are likely to be available on a CD-ROM, and most computer magazines giving away software do so largely via CDs), but the drawback is that CD-ROMs are not writable. This makes them ideal for software manufacturers to use as installation disks, or for computer magazines to bundle free software on, since they hold much more information than floppy disks, and are unlikely to get damaged in transit; but if you want to swap a file with someone else, you will still have to resort to the humble, writable floppy – unless you have a writable WORM CD-R drive, and the CDs to go with it. WORM stands for *Write Once, Read Many (times)*: you can record information on a CD-R *(Compact Disk-Recordable)*, and access it as often as you want, but you cannot erase or replace data that you have recorded: it is burnt into the recordable surface of the disk, and cannot be altered. Consequently, you have to be very careful about what you record on such a CD – and this may discourage some people from using them, preferring instead to use the more forgiving floppy disk.

Nevertheless, for many purposes, such as backups of very important files that are unlikely to be updated often, writable CDs offer an ideal alternative to floppy disks.

Backup drive

If you find that you need to back up important data regularly from your hard disk, then buying a backup drive may be the answer. You can either have a tape unit, usually built-in to the system unit, or purchase a removable hard disk drive (sometimes called a zip drive after the brand name created by the market leader Iomega). A tape backup unit uses special data cartridges which are sophisticated versions of your audio cassette tapes.

Modern backup drives bundled with the appropriate software are very fast and ideal for backing up either your whole hard disk, or selective directories/files.

Joystick

Instead of using the mouse and the keyboard, a joystick is an alternative way of interacting with your computer.

It is usually used to play games. You'll see some PCs with a special "games" port at the back of the system unit into which the joystick connector is plugged.

Graphics tablet

Instead of using a mouse, a graphics tablet is used for advanced drawing applications where accuracy is critical. For example, *Computer Aided Design* (CAD) applications.

Plotter

For specialised applications where ouput is required on a much larger format paper than standard paper sizes used in a normal printer.

Ports

There are two types of ports at the back of the system unit to connect various peripheral devices: serial and parallel. Ensure that your new system has at least two serial and one parallel ports.

A parallel port is for communication in one direction only (output) and therefore it is commonly used to connect the printer. It can transmit information in parallel along a multi-wired cable so it's faster compared to a standard serial port.

Serial ports, although generally slower than parallel ports, are bi-directional. They are often labelled as *COM1* and *COM2*. Typical devices connected to serial ports include modems and scanners. Some printers and mice also use them.

With the advent of the Internet and the popularity of fast modems most new PCs are now fitted with faster serial ports.

Expansion slots

A PC is designed so that it can be expanded easily: increase memory, add additional devices, communicate with the outside world.

This expansion capability is catered for by expansion slots found at the back when you take the cover off your system unit case. There are usually at least five spare expansion slots provided. When you have a need to expand your basic system then appropriate expansion cards can be purchased and slotted into place. Examples of expansion cards include: network cards, video/graphics card, internal modem card.

Power supply unit (PSU)

This is inside the system unit and it converts your mains power supply into low voltage DC supply to power the whole of your computer system.

If suddenly the power supply is taken away, anything that you may have been working on at the time and not saved, will be lost. Accidents can sometimes happen: the office cleaner could unplug the computer power cable to use the same socket for the vacuum cleaner, someone may trip over the computer power cable, there may be a failure at the supply end or lightning may strike. To safeguard against any of these you can buy a UPS *(Uninterruptable Power Supply)* unit. This uses a special battery that will ensure that a constant supply of current is maintained to your PC when there is a power failure.This reserve power will last long enough for you to save your work properly and shut down the computer safely.

Types of PCs

Confused by the wide range of PCs on the market? Perhaps it would help if you just think of them as very sophisticated and expensive calculators – all made to perform the same functions.

What varies between various models is the speed, capacity and portability. Obviously, a faster machine is going to cost more. If you are going to use a PC for top-end serious applications then you will need one that can cope with large storage capacity. If you need to use a PC from various locations then you will want to buy a lightweight portable.

The major part of the PC that determines its capabilities is the micro chip used for its processor. When looking at a PC specification you will notice the term MHz listed as part of the processor type. E.g. Pentium 200MHz. This is the actual speed rating given to the chip. MHz stands for Megahertz and means millions of pulses per second. Hence, 200 MHz means 200 million pulses per second. A PC has an internal clock that sends out millions of pulses per second. Each instruction executed by a PC uses up several pulses but the higher the number of pulses per second, the faster the PC can execute the instruction. So a Pentium with 200 MHz will be faster than a Pentium with 166 MHz.

A broad classification of PCs on the market today is:

- Desktop – designed to be placed on your desk and expected to remain there for most of the time.
- Notebook – aims to satisfy users who are on the move a lot and need a PC that they can move around easily.

Desktop

This is the most popular type available. Although the system unit case is often placed on the desk, you can purchase tower case systems which are floor-standing and can fit neatly under your desk or beside it. Only the monitor, keyboard and the mouse then strictly need to be placed on the desktop. Although tower cases are a little more expensive the advantages are clear: more room on your desk, more space inside the case so it's convenient to upgrade system unit components, and usually extra expansion slots are available at the back too.

Notebook

By definition a notebook should be the same length and width as the standard A4 size paper, but obviously quite a bit thicker. It should be able to fit in a standard briefcase. Present day notebooks do, but leave little room for anything else you may wish to carry. Notebooks are now much more common than the earlier laptops which were a bit bigger and heavier.

Notebooks run from the mains or on rechargeable batteries, lasting as little as forty-five minutes to over six hours. The battery life depends largely on how hard it has to work to process your data. Frequent disk accesses, for instance, will use more battery power. Before the battery is about to run out a 'battery low' indicator will appear – use this warning to ensure that all your work is saved before power is lost completely. Most notebooks now use Nickel metal hydride and Lithium ion batteries in preference to the older NiCad batteries.

The keyboards have fewer keys than the standard PC keyboard. Some keys are used for more than one character. Instead of a mouse, a pointing device is incorporated into the case, like a trackball or more commonly now a trackpad.

Also, most modern notebooks have a CD-ROM drive, a PC card slot into which you can plug various credit-card sized expansion cards for a faxmodem, extra hard disk, or even networking. Faster and sharper TFT *(Thin Film Transfer)* screens are becoming standard over the older liquid crystal display (LCD) technology used in DSTN *(Double SuperTwisted Nematic)* screens. Generally though, a notebook specification is still lower than an equivalent desktop but the cost is greater. You should therefore only buy a notebook if you *really* need portability.

Software

Software is the most important part of a computer system. It enables you to draft a letter, perform calculations or manage your information. Your computer or hardware is of little use without software. A computer system without software is like a complete music system, including speakers and amplifier, but without any music tapes or CDs. Your music system can be very sophisticated and expensive, but without any music to play on it, it is of little use.

So what is software exactly? It is a program or a collection of programs written to enable your computer to perform a useful task. A program is made up of special commands and statements that are obeyed and executed by your computer. A computer cannot do anything that it has not been programmed to do.

Types of software

There are thousands of commercial software packages available for the PC today. They range from simple games programs to complex applications. New and better software packages are being developed every day. We will look at the main categories of software in this section and discuss the important features and benefits they offer.

The main categories of software are:

- Word processors
- Spreadsheets
- Databases
- Accounting/Personal finance
- Graphics
  - Drawing and Painting
  - Presentation
  - CAD
- Desktop publishing (DTP)
- Integrated software
- Utilities
- Internet software
- Multimedia:
  - Education
  - Reference
  - Entertainment
- Development tools

Word processors

A PC-based word processor package is far superior to the traditional typewriter. Even the market for expensive dedicated word processor machines was wiped out, almost overnight, after general word processing software came on the scene. Today there are many individuals and companies purchasing PCs primarily for creating documents.

Word processors are different because you can easily change your text as often as you want before printing the final document. You can edit on-screen, reposition blocks of text, specify automatic centring or straight right margin, search for specific words and replace them automatically, create a standard header and a footer (with page numbers, say), and so on.

As well as the standard facilities mentioned above, current word processors offer other features like:

Spelling and Grammar checker

Checks either all your spellings and grammar on-the-fly or specific words against an on-line dictionary.

Thesaurus

Allows you to see synonyms (words with similar meanings) so that you can decide on words best suited.

Auto-save

Saves your document onto disk automatically at a given time interval. This is especially important if you are typing in a long document and don't want to risk losing it all.

Mail-merge

Enables you to combine two files. It is usually used to merge a file containing names and addresses with a standard letter to create personalised letters.

WYSIWYG

Pronounced "wizzy-wig". It stands for "what you see is what you get" and means that when you use special printing effects like **bold** and <u>underlining</u>, you'll be able to see these on the screen exactly as they appear when printed.

Print preview

Sometimes called page preview. It allows you to see the complete page with all the formatting including margins, headers and footers, on one screen. It saves you wasting paper and time because you know what your printed page is going to look like before you commit yourself to printing it.

Macros

If you need to type the same long piece of text, or you

need to perform the same key operations frequently, you can specify these once in a macro. Then, assign a function key, like F12, to your macro. Every time you want to repeat the sequence of commands or to type the same piece of text, simply press F12.

Indexing and Table of Contents

Advanced word processors can automatically generate a table of contents and an index with page numbers. You can specify or mark the words you want and the word processor will do the rest. If you edit your document, you can simply ask your word processor to regenerate the index.

Import and Export

Often there is a requirement to read a file from another word processor or a spreadsheet (importing) and to output the documents you create into other formats (exporting).

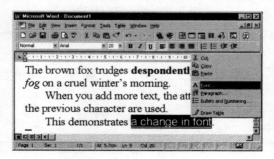

Spreadsheets

Many businesses and individuals purchased PCs purely to be able to use a spreadsheet.

A spreadsheet can be thought of as a large calculator, used to solve any numerical problem that can be presented in rows and columns. It allows much greater flexibility because you can mix numbers, formulas and text. One great benefit of using a spreadsheet is to be able to perform **"what if"** analysis.

For example, John Smith wants to arrange a suitable overdraft facility with his bank. Let us assume that purchases are 50% of sales and variable costs are 10% of sales. This information can easily be entered in a spreadsheet and derived figures will be calculated automatically, as shown here. We can also see that John

	A	B	C	D	E	F	G
1	**John Smith - Cash Flow Jan-Jun 1998**						
2							
3		Jan-98	Feb-98	Mar-98	Apr-98	May-98	Jun-98
4							
5	**Opening Bank Balance**	-3000	-2000	-2600	-2800	200	4800
6							
7	**Sales Receipts**	10000	6000	7000	15000	19000	24000
8							
9	Purchase Payments	5000	3000	3500	7500	9500	12000
10	Variable Costs Payments	1000	600	700	1500	1900	2400
11	Fixed Costs Payments	3000	3000	3000	3000	3000	3000
12	**Total Outflow**	9000	6600	7200	12000	14400	17400
13							
14	**Closing Bank Balance**	-2000	-2600	-2800	200	4800	11400

Smith needs to arrange an overdraft facility until April 1998. Now, what if, sales receipts in just the first month were to drop to £5,000. By making this single change, as shown here, the spreadsheet will recalculate all related

	A	B	C	D	E	F	G
1	John Smith - Cash Flow Jan-Jun 1998						
2							
3		Jan-98	Feb-98	Mar-98	Apr-98	May-98	Jun-98
4							
5	**Opening Bank Balance**	-3000	-4000	-4600	-4800	-1800	2800
6							
7	**Sales Receipts**	5000	6000	7000	15000	19000	24000
8							
9	Purchase Payments	2500	3000	3500	7500	9500	12000
10	Variable Costs Payments	500	600	700	1500	1900	2400
11	Fixed Costs Payments	3000	3000	3000	3000	3000	3000
12	**Total Outflow**	6000	6600	7200	12000	14400	17400
13							
14	**Closing Bank Balance**	-4000	-4600	-4800	-1800	2800	9400

figures instantly, at the touch of a button. You can also see that the overdraft will be required for an additional month.

This is a very simple example to make the point. You can make it more realistic by incorporating bank interest, breakdown of expenses, breakdown of sales by product and so on. In brief, once you have your raw data in a spreadsheet, you can have any number of scenarios, no matter how complex they might be. You can use a spreadsheet for repetitive accounting tasks or as a tool for management decision making.

Some of the specific features offered by spreadsheets include:

Formulas

All spreadsheets provide simple mathematical operations like subtraction and division from which you can build complex formulas yourself. Most spreadsheets also provide specialised functions and formulas to save you time. These include:

Mathematical	Average, Count, Maximum, Minimum, Sum
Trigonometric	Sine, Cosine, Tangent, Pi
Logical	And, Or, Not
Date	Date, Time
Statistical	Standard Deviation, Variance
Financial	Compound Interest, Rate of Return on Investment

These built-in formulas make it much easier for you to build financial models using your spreadsheet.

Macros

These are very important for automating repetitive procedures within a spreadsheet. You can execute a macro representing several keystrokes or commands by simply pressing a function key. They can speed up your work and make life much easier. Macros can also be used to customise your spreadsheet for specific applications.

Graphics

It is sometimes much easier to understand a single picture or a graph rather than a mass of numbers. Good spreadsheets can instantly create business graphics from basic numerical data. Now your "what if" analysis can not only show the effects numerically, but also graphically.

Linking

Instead of creating one enormous spreadsheet for the whole company, it is much easier to work with several smaller ones and link them. Changing a value in one spreadsheet will automatically recalculate all related values in other spreadsheets that are linked.

Multi-Dimensional

Say you wanted to record Sales by Salesmen and by Area. Normally, you'd have to create two spreadsheets; one for Sales by Salesmen and another one for Sales by Area and then link them. An alternative is to create one three-dimensional spreadsheet to record Sales, Salesmen and Area details. You can then even produce a three-dimensional graph from it.

Databases

A database is a collection of data, called a file, stored in a computer. Examples include mailing lists, customer records and employee data. A database management system (DBMS), commonly called a database too, is a software package allowing you to store, manipulate and retrieve data. A database is different from a spreadsheet because it allows you to record the current 'real' state of your business rather than future projections.

A database is often described as an electronic card-file. A database record is equivalent to a card. The individual pieces of information on a card, like name, address, telephone number, are known as fields within a record. Databases that replicate the card-file exactly are known as flat-file databases.

The real power of databases is only realised in a relational database management system (RDBMS). A relational database package allows you to have many tables or databases – each capable of joining with another to provide powerful cross-referencing. It also avoids duplication of data. Relational databases are more sophisticated. Almost every database software supplier has jumped on the 'relational-band-wagon' – claiming to be offering a relational solution. It is therefore wise, when choosing your system, to look closely at the features offered, rather than relying solely on the relational label.

Some of the main features to look for include:

Ease of use

It must be easy to create and modify databases. You should also be able to input new information and display it easily.

Indexing

This is a way of accessing a record or several records within a large database quickly. It is a technique similar to the one we use when we search the index of a book to find the relevant pages. In the database context, a new file is created and it represents an index to the main database file.

Relations

Quite often you will need to create several files, and link them with a relation. A relation is where there is a record in each file with common attributes and so a link can be formed. An example is a customer file forming a relation with an orders file on customer number.

Manipulation

Once you have created your database and entered information in it, you need a facility to manipulate the data to reap maximum benefits. This is done by:

- functions like COUNT, MAXIMUM, MINIMUM to operate on the data. These are similar to those provided in a spreadsheet.
- a programming environment. For example, the Visual Basic programming language can be used with the Access database.
- a facility to submit queries to the database. A standard query language is SQL *(Structured Query Language)*. Some packages offer a Query-By-Example facility too. This is a simple form on your screen that you fill and the query is automatically generated from it.

Screens and Menus

It is fine to use the default screen to input data initially. However, it is much better to be able to design your own screens for data-entry and manipulation. You should be able to place fields anywhere on the screen, draw boxes, type headings and so on. Customised menus will allow you to use different parts of your system and link your screens together.

Reports and Labels

A report generator should allow you to format your report easily. You should be able to test the report with a print preview before printing it on paper. A label generator is a common requirement from a database. You should be able to specify the format of your labels and again print preview them with actual data before committing to final printing.

As well as the facilities described, check that it is easy to make changes to the structure of your database, even after you have entered data. The database should not slow down as you input more data and it should offer on-screen help.

Choosing the right database package to start with is perhaps more important than for any other type of software. This is because once you have created your complete application (screens, reports, programs), and input data, it is difficult to make major changes or to make it conform to another database software package. Many database software companies provide a demonstration disk of virtually the full product, so that you can evaluate their product thoroughly before making a decision to buy it. You are just limited in the number of records you can create.

Accounting/Personal finance

An accounting system is one application of a database system. It is possible to write your own accounting system from a database if you are technically inclined and have the time. It is also possible to use a spreadsheet, especially for small businesses, rather than to buy a full blown accounts system. For most, it is far easier to purchase an off-the-shelf accounts (or personal finance) package.

A personal finance package, like Quicken or Microsoft Money, differs from a business accounting system in that it is aimed primarily at the home user to aid in planning and budgeting for the home. You can monitor liabilities like mortgages, car loans, as well as investments like pensions and shares. It can help you save for major goals like school fees or holidays. Also, newer packages integrate on-line banking and the Internet.

If you are a business user, then you may opt for Sage Sterling. This package integrates Sales, Purchase and Nominal ledgers. Other basic facilities provided include:

- Invoice production and credit note facility
- Bank payment and petty cash
- Reports: VAT return, account history, debt-chasing letters, budgets, audit trial, Profit and Loss report, Balance sheet

Quite often you can also purchase additional modules if you need to extend the basic accounting system. Examples include stock control, Job costing and Payroll. If you purchase a payroll system you should make sure that you will receive updates whenever the Government changes PAYE and NIC regulations.

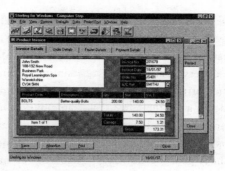

Graphics

Graphics have now become standard on all modern computers. Most word processors, spreadsheets and databases offer a graphics capability. These packages allow you to produce standard business graphs. They include Bar charts, Pie charts, X-Y line graphs, 3D graphs and so on.

If your requirement is more specific, you may need to buy a dedicated graphics package, which can be split into three basic types:

- Drawing and Painting
- Presentation
- CAD

Drawing and Painting

These are a substitute for either a pencil or a paintbrush.

They allow you to create free-hand line drawings (Drawing programs) and you can fill an area with colour (Painting programs). Some products, like CorelDRAW below, combine both these functions.

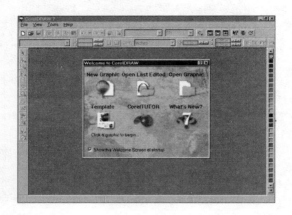

Since most of us are not artists, these packages often come with a library of cliparts. These are drawings already created by someone else. You can simply copy them and make modifications if necessary.

Presentation

These packages specialise in producing graphics on overhead projector foils or on 35mm photographic slides. You can even turn your PC into a slide projector – each picture will be displayed in turn on your screen after a key-press or a short time delay.

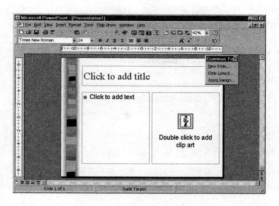

CAD

These are special types of programs used for complex technical drawings. It stands for Computer Aided Design.

If precision and accuracy are very important than a CAD program is required. Examples of use include designing a car or a building.

Desktop publishing

Desktop publishing (DTP) is a way of integrating text and graphics on the same page. DTP will allow you to use your PC for producing high quality brochures, newsletters, books, magazines and other types of documents.

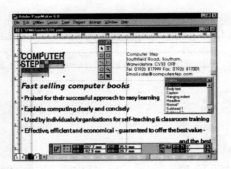

DTP on the PC today is far more cost effective than traditional typesetting. It saves countless hours on manual cut-and-paste, corrections and general layout. To get into DTP, the most important requirement is choosing the right software. DTP software on its own, however, will not do everything. You will still need a word processor for typing in the text; a graphics package, and perhaps a scanner if you need to scan pictures or images into your document.

When choosing DTP software, make sure it is compatible with other software and hardware you plan to use with it. You may also decide to invest in a laser printer for high-quality output.

Some important features that DTP software can offer include:

Drop cap

This is a large capital letter occupying several lines. It is usually used to start the first paragraph in a chapter, as seen in this book.

Guidlines

These are horizontal and vertical lines you can set on a page layout to align text or graphics accurately.

Kerning

Allows you to reduce the gap between certain pairs of characters so that they are not all evenly spaced out. This can make large important headlines more pleasing and easier to read. For example between 'W'-and-'A'.

Tracking

This alters spacing between all letters and words in the main body of the text – from very tight to very loose.

Master pages

These pages do not print, but anything placed in them will normally appear on other pages as a fixed background. For example: a logo, heading or footer line with page numbers. Master pages enable you to easily create a consistent design for your document.

Cropping graphics

You can "chop-off" any bit of an imported graphic, like a photograph.

Text wrap

This is applied to graphic objects to create either a fixed standoff boundary before text is wrapped around it (regular wrap), or you can create an irregular wrap, where the text follows the shape of an irregularly-shaped graphic (with curves, etc.).

Integrated software

Instead of buying a separate software package for each function you can just buy one integrated package. An integrated package can provide a combination of the following:

- Word Processor
- Spreadsheet
- Database
- Communication
- Graphics
- Desktop accessories (such as calculator, diary)

An example of a low-end package is Microsoft Works. This provides major cost savings when compared to buying a word processor, a spreadsheet, etc. separately.

If you require serious business software, then the latest version of Microsoft Office, Lotus SmartSuite or Corel Office may be the answer. These combine leading individual components (also sold separately) into one integrated product, so that it's more competitively priced. You are also likely to find that if you are buying a new PC, one of these integrated packages is bundled in free.

Utilities

Utility software enables you to work with your PC more easily. You can have a utility to:

- Uninstall an application completely from your PC
- Compress files to reduce the number of backup floppy disks
- Backup and Restore files
- Recover corrupted files
- Organise your hard disk
- Encrypt or protect important files

Some utilities just perform one task, whilst others may perform a combination of chores. You'll find that many of these functions will be available from your Windows operating system, so you may never need to buy a dedicated utility software package.

Internet software

The growth of the Internet has brought with it an increasing amount of software designed to make the navigation of it easier and more effective. This software includes Web browsers and other Internet client programs, e-mail readers, HTML authoring programs, encryption utilities, etc. Most Internet software can be downloaded from the Internet itself, and some of it is shareware (see later). You'll also find that the latest applications (word processor, DTP, graphics, etc.) all provide features to generate Internet web pages and easy links to the 'net. Windows itself makes Internet access easy. This subject is covered in detail in Section 5: *The Internet*.

Multimedia

Before true multimedia came along, specialist computer programs had for some years been available that were dedicated to performing tasks such as playing and recording music, showing video clips, and playing games. Multimedia is the name given to the concept of bringing together a collection of these and other media, in order to provide an artificial environment in which to learn, create, relax and play.

The concept of multimedia has been around for several years, but until recently the necessary computer technology was not available (at least to the ordinary home or business user), especially in terms of the system requirements (e.g. hard drive space, RAM, monitor resolution) needed for a computer to deal speedily and effectively with the combination of tasks required of it.

Today, however, you would be unlikely to buy a hard drive of less than 1 gigabyte, RAM is very cheap, and most monitors can handle high-resolution images quickly. Most important, however, is the current availability of cheap, fast CD-ROM drives, and the software to support them. Video clips and sound recordings take up a lot of storage space, on both the medium on which they are shipped, and the medium on which they are stored on your computer (if different). Whereas a floppy disk, still the most popular removable storage medium, can hold 1.44 megabytes, a CD can hold at least 660 Mb.

Some of the main areas where multimedia software is popular today include:

Education

Even in the earliest days of information technology, it was realised that computers were ideally suited to aiding learning in certain situations. For instance, if a student needs to be tested repeatedly on a limited number of criteria, as when a more-or-less constant set of principles (such as a language's grammatical rules) have to be acquired, a computer can perform this task repeatedly, for as long as the student wants, without getting bored or frustrated or having to attend to other duties. Multimedia education titles have the advantage that they can pool together lots of different types of information and present it in the best form (animation, video, sound, graphics, text) to provide a truly magnificent learning experience. A good example of this is the Dorling Kindersley Children's Dictionary. This is designed for children aged between 7-12 and teaches them to spell and pronounce thousands of words in an exciting way.

Reference

Additionally, computers can be used as a reference material. In the past, when computers were mostly text-based, there was little point in anyone choosing to read from a screen rather than from a book – books are easier on the eye, they can contain detailed illustrations, and can be used for reference on virtually every aspect of human knowledge, whereas the amount of information that exists in a form that can be accessed by computers is comparatively limited. However, with the development of multimedia technology, all this has changed. Whereas a book might include an illustration of, say, a cutaway section of an internal combustion engine, a multimedia CD-ROM application could show the same engine as an animation, illustrating the way the different parts move. Furthermore, the facility for cross-referencing is greatly improved. Whereas a book has to rely on an index, page references and footnotes, the text of a multimedia encyclopedia contains highlighted topics which can be clicked on with a mouse pointer to jump immediately to the appropriate section.

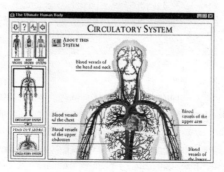

One of the most irritating things about browsing through a book encyclopedia is the fact that, in following a line of enquiry, moving from one cross-referenced topic to another, it is very easy to get sidetracked and forget what you wanted to learn about in the first place. Multimedia encyclopedias such as Microsoft's Encarta offers Back and Next buttons (much like the ones available from Internet Web browsers) – so it is easy to select any topic that you chose not to follow earlier on.

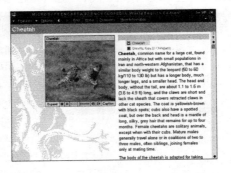

Even where multimedia functions are not appropriate, as in a dictionary, computer reference materials can offer vast improvements over simple books. For example, the Oxford English Dictionary, currently comprising around half a million words, can be bought on a single CD-ROM. The search capabilities of its user interface are enormous. For example, a language scholar wanting to study the development of a word through history might spend years poring over the book version of the dictionary, and even then miss out important references due to natural human oversight. The search engine used by the CD-ROM version, however, could find every instance of the word in the dictionary in a matter of seconds. The references produced then have to be analysed and made sense of, but the scholar is relieved of doing a significant amount of donkey-work.

However, a CD-ROM, or any future data storage medium, no matter how much the data is compressed, can only hold a restricted amount of information. The World-Wide Web, on the other hand, allows the user to access a virtually unlimited wealth of information. This information can be updated immediately as required, and does not have to wait for the development of packaging and marketing campaigns before the user can access it. Admittedly, Web pages are often not subjected to any form of quality control, and may not present information in the most didactically effective way possible – while a CD-ROM such as Encarta will have been edited, reorganised and improved in order to make it a saleable product. At any rate, while telephone bills are still expensive, and the Web is full of such a large degree of mediocre or useless material, self-contained reference software will continue to be the best choice for certain requirements.

Or perhaps you want to plan your road journey on a PC using AutoRoute Express. AutoRoute Express is another useful package that provides a map and a detailed table of driving directions of any journey. It allows you to select the quickest time, shortest distance, or the most scenic route whenever you want to travel from one place to another.

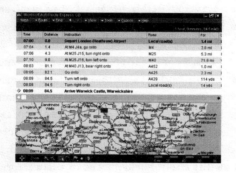

AutoRoute Express also contains information on sights you may want to visit, hotels, restaurants and campsites. There are even photographs on many of the favourite destinations.

Entertainment

While dedicated games consoles are enormously popular, and ideally suited for those who are happy with playing platform games and racing car simulators, they are very restricted in the type of entertainment they can provide, and only allow the user to interact with the system via a joystick or control pad with two or three buttons. A PC, while considerably more expensive, is a much more versatile system, capable of entertaining the whole family. You can use it to play action games, take part in adventures that require you to use your brain, or explore virtual worlds.

One great advantage of the multimedia explosion is the fact that the line between education and entertainment is often becoming increasingly blurred. For instance, browsing through Encarta (mentioned earlier) can be a very exciting and entertaining experience; learning need no longer be a chore for those who find books dull and oppressive. Similarly, many pieces of software that are ostensibly games include some educational content, as in children's adventure games, where a list of principles or facts might have to be discovered in order to earn points or win a prize. This has given rise to the term *edutainment*, now a rather hackneyed buzzword, which will hopefully fall into disuse as improved multimedia learning environments make it unnecessary to specify that a means of education is also entertaining.

One favourite sports game enjoyed by many is Microsoft Golf. You can play it on your PC whatever the weather!

Development tools

These differ somewhat from the software mentioned above, in that they are used to create other pieces of software. While your PC at the most basic level deals with '1's and '0's, programmers do not create software by typing lines of binary code. All software is written using a programming language, which acts as an interface between the programmer and the computer. Such languages include C, Delphi, Visual Basic and Java.

While most PC users are unlikely ever to have the need to use a programming language, it is useful to know what these languages are if you come across their names. Development tools differ greatly in terms of the environment used to enter commands. At one end of the spectrum there are 'low-level' languages, or assemblers, which interact directly with the computer's central processor: these produce very efficient, compact routines, but are composed of abstract commands which are difficult to learn.

At the other end of the spectrum are 'high-level' languages: these offer a more friendly environment in which to program, using intuitive commands, but the complex interface that fills the wide gap between programmer and processor produces larger, less streamlined programs. An example of a high-level language, and the one you are most likely to hear mentioned, is Visual Basic, which is used to create Windows applications by using a graphical interface. Instead of entering lines of code in a text editor, the user can create windows, buttons, menus, etc. – all the elements that you find in the Windows environment – by clicking on toolbar buttons and placing the elements where they are wanted. Visual Basic then translates these into a sequence of simple commands that can subsequently be edited manually. When an application is working satisfactorily, it can be compiled into an executable file, which can be run by anyone you distribute it to – as long as they have a special run-time module on their computer.

If you are interested in developing software, Visual Basic is certainly the most user-friendly tool to use, and the easiest to get to grips with – but many professional programmers prefer the superior efficiency of C (there is a Visual C++ product similar to Visual Basic) or Delphi (an object-oriented language, like Visual Basic, but more advanced).

As the Internet becomes ever more important, new programming environments are needed that can take advantage of Internet technology and resources. One such language, developed by Sun Microsystems, is Java. This allows the programmer to create small, effective applications called *applets* that can be transmitted easily over the Internet and used to perform special functions on the user's remote computer. Microsoft's new Internet development technology is known as *ActiveX*, and offers the option of integration with many other Microsoft products, such as Office. ActiveX is designed to help incorporate multimedia, virtual reality and animation into a unified computer environment where there is no vital distinction between the resources of the user's computer and those of the Internet.

Shareware and Public Domain

Shareware is an interesting marketing concept used to promote sales of software. It allows you to try the software before you decide to buy it. All you need to pay initially is the cost of a disk and handling. Basic documentation on how to use the program is provided as a computer file too. You are trusted to register the program if you decide to keep on using it. Once you have paid the registration fee, you will normally receive an upgraded version of the product, full documentation manuals and technical support. The Internet offers a lot of shareware software you can download for free.

Public Domain (PD) software is slightly different. You can use it as often as you please without ever paying any money to the authors.

Viruses

A computer virus is a man-made electronic disease. It can corrupt files on your PC and wipe off important data. It can strike at any time. Even when you least expect it.

So what is a virus exactly? It is a piece of software designed to cause severe destruction to important information on your PC. It is often designed to be transmitted easily from one PC to another without being detected. This spreading of viruses is particularly easy if you use floppy disks for information exchange, or if your PC is linked to others, via either a local network or the Internet. The Internet is the ideal channel of communication for viruses: thousands of computers all around the world, linked to each other via an anarchic network over which no single person or organisation has any control. Viruses and the Internet are discussed in Section 5: *The Internet*.

To detect viruses and to kill them, you can buy anti-virus toolkits. However, none can guarantee to detect all viruses – new ones are continually produced. Other precautions you should take include:

- Do not try software from dubious sources
- Be careful who you let loose on your PC
- Take regular backups of your data and software

Shopping

T his section takes you through the stages involved in choosing and buying your hardware and software – in other words, your system. It also gives you detailed guidelines on using various sources for finding relevant information before making a purchasing decision.

To choose the right system you should consider the following steps:

What will I need my PC for?

Before you venture any further, work out in your mind why exactly you want to buy a PC. It is quite surprising how many people buy a PC without having a clear idea about what they want to do with it. Then they get disappointed when they realise that their machine is not powerful enough to run the software they need. Do you want a PC for a serious application such as word-processing or accounting for your business? Do you want a PC for entertainment purposes or do you want to buy a PC for educational purposes? Perhaps you want a PC for all of these reasons. For instance, you may want a word processor at home for writing letters and some educational software for your children. But, your spouse rather likes the idea of playing a game of golf on it. Perhaps you also have a more specialised requirement such as composing music.

What's available?

Once you have identified why you want a PC, you need to find out what is available in the market to meet your requirements. The latter part of this section looks at how to find information on various products. This part discusses the factors to consider when looking through this information:

Features

Study and compare all the features offered by competing products. Do they provide all the features you may need? Do any of the products offer any exceptional features?

Price

Obviously, the more sophisticated a product is, the higher the price tag. A laser printed output is quite attractive, but do you really need it to write letters to your bank manager? Similarly, the latest version of Word is not a necessity if you are just going to use your PC to write formal letters. However, if you are buying a PC to write a book or to write customer proposals, then, your minimum requirements may be a laser printer and an advanced word processor.

Compatibility

As mentioned in the last section, software is the most important part of your system. First, you need to decide on the software packages you intend using. Then, find out their minimum system requirements. These will include factors such as: memory, hard disk and processing speed. Make sure that the hardware you buy will easily be able to run all your software. You also need to allow for extra hard disk storage for your data.

Learning curve

The more advanced a product is, the longer it takes to learn to use it. Some of the expensive software offers advanced features. However, simple functions may be

difficult to find and use. You may want to buy software
that is familiar to you. If you are buying a PC to do extra
work at home, you may want to buy the same software
that you use at work to shorten your learning curve.

Reliability

When buying a PC for serious business applications,
avoid computer hardware that has been known to have
problems. Software does not suddenly fail, but it may
contain 'bugs'. A software bug is when the program does
not behave as expected in certain circumstances. For
serious applications, such as business accounting, avoid
first releases of new products, unless they have been
available for quite some time. With complex applications
it takes quite a while before all the bugs are found and
eliminated. Although these bugs are not always serious,
as a new computer user you want to steer clear from all
known problems, no matter how minor they may be.

Budgeting

Once you have a fair idea of how much a personal
computer system can cost, you can plan how much you
want to spend on each individual part. When budgeting,
start with the essentials. For a small business, these may
be: an accounting software package that can generate

invoices, a printer that allows you to print on continuous stationery and a PC with a 1 Gigabyte hard disk. Work out how much these items will cost. Add the cost of small accessories like printer cables. If you have any funds left in your budget, then you can go for little luxuries such as a higher resolution screen.

Obtaining the best deal

Getting the best deal means finding a good price as well as reasonable support. Don't just look for the lowest price. Look for a reliable and helpful supplier. Check that all products carry a vendor's warranty against defects in workmanship. Generally, computer hardware is guaranteed for twelve months against any faults that may develop and technical problems you may encounter. Whereas, with software you generally get free technical support for a few months. After this period you have to buy your support.

If you buy the total system from one company you may be able to negotiate a good price or get some freebies. Be careful when a computer dealer tells you that he is giving you free software with your computer. Quite often computer manufacturers bundle popular software with their PCs. Check that the dealer is giving away what he claims.

When it comes to finding information on computer products, you want to start from independent sources (i.e. those who do not sell computer products), such as product reviews in computer magazines. Your friends and colleagues can also be good independent sources – if they don't sell computers for a living. Once you are fairly confident with the lingo and know how to compare different products, then approach computer dealers for detailed information and advice.

Use these sources to choose (and buy) your computer:

Computer magazines

The next step after reading this book is to find information on various computer products. Start by reading leading computer magazines. Do this even before you approach your local dealer. Although you will need to spend some time reading, you will avoid getting confused by computer dealers or being misled into buying the wrong system.

Types available

The main categories of PC magazines for end users can be defined by the type of readers they are aimed at:

General consumers and beginners

These magazines cover issues concerning all PC users. They can be purchased at most newsagents.

Professionals in large organisations

These look at issues relating specifically to large companies. Most are available by free subscriptions to anyone with an authority to purchase systems or to influence purchasing decisions within an organisation.

Small/medium size business owners

These are available by subscriptions only. As well as covering topics relating to PCs, these magazines cover various business issues.

Technical users

Covers technical topics such as programming.

For your purpose of choosing a computer system, magazines available in newsagents are appropriate.

Product reviews

One main function of these magazines is to review all major products being released in the market. Most reviews are independent from product vendors. Unlike your local computer dealers, the magazine writers when reviewing products, are not trying to sell to you. Also, because they see and review many products, they are able to provide a fair judgement.

Product reviews usually consist of a detailed description of the features offered by the product, followed by the reviewer's opinion and general ratings on factors such as ease of use, functionality, documentation, speed and value for money. More useful reviews also provide a comparison between competing products. Almost all reviews state where to get more information or where to buy the products.

To play it safe, you should read at least two or three reviews on a specific product. You may also contact the vendors to obtain copies of reviews on their products. They will be pleased to send you these, especially if the reviews are favourable. Quite often, it is interesting to read letters that follow a review in subsequent issues. Letters from readers, vendors and competitors often reveal interesting facts that have been overlooked by the reviewer.

Advertisements

Just like advertisements for any other products, advertisements in computer magazines are designed to attract your attention rather than to be informative. Nevertheless, do make a point of looking at these. They will, at least, tell you how to get further information. Almost all ads have a coupon or a telephone number you can use for further information.

Advertisements can also reveal something about the company and the success of their products. If you see a new ad in every computer magazine and it disappears after a short time, then it usually means that the campaign was not successful and the product did not achieve anticipated sales. You should perhaps think twice before rushing into buying this product! Also look at the positioning of the ad. Prime positions such as the back cover and front inside cover are the most expensive in the magazine. Usually, it is the larger companies that tend to pay the premium prices for these pages. These companies are more likely to be around for a long time and provide you with support. After these prime positions, come the first few pages of the magazine. These are fairly prominent positions too – and so is the price. Have you ever wondered why the Contents page in magazines is never the first page? Now you know! Magazine publishers are better off selling the page and making it a revenue earner rather than using it themselves.

Some magazines offer a reader enquiry service, whereby you just send off one card to the publishers, indicating the products that interest you from those advertised and reviewed. Using this service to get more information is easier than to write to each individual vendor. Although, it is much slower – be prepared to wait quite a bit longer to receive the details requested.

Some advertisers will encourage you to buy directly from the details provided on an ad page. This is usually the case with low-priced products. You can usually place orders over the telephone by using a credit card to pay for the purchase.

Other companies that tend to advertise heavily to get your orders over the phone are computer dealers offering leading branded products at reduced prices. Some of these dealers survive by selling very large volumes. They have to put all their efforts into selling, to achieve high unit sales. Therefore, they have less time to provide any technical advice or support. Buy from these dealers once you know what you want.

One thing to remember when answering these advertisements is that when you request details from companies, your name and address will be added to their customer database. If you use the magazine's reader enquiry service, your details will also be added to the publisher's database. This is not as bad as it sounds. It allows them to send you updated information on their products. If, however, you are very concerned about receiving "junk mail", you can ask them not to use the personal details you provide for any other purpose.

Reader offers

Some consumer computer magazines sell products to their readers at special prices. The magazine publishers act like mail order computer dealers; they buy goods from vendors and sell them to end users. The only difference is that the publishers are much more choosy about the products they sell. The products they offer are typically low-priced and have been recommended in their reviews.

As the term "reader offer" implies, the products are sold at discounted prices to the readers. You send your order by mail; either send a cheque or give your credit card number. Some magazines also offer a telephone ordering service to make it easy for you to order.

Customer support for these products is provided by the vendors. The magazines' reader-offer staff are not really geared towards giving technical advice or resolving technical problems.

So you can use this service to find bargains and feel comfortable that the products you are buying are commendable.

Again, when you buy products from the publisher, or subscribe to their magazine, your details will be maintained on their customer database. So don't be surprised when you regularly start receiving details on subscribing to their other magazines or buying other products. Some publishers also "rent out" their customer database. This means that they give a copy of their customer database, or a selection from it, to other companies at a nominal charge. Companies paying for this list can send a mailshot to addresses on the list once. They cannot take another copy or keep a copy. If they want to use the same list again, they have to make another payment to the list owner. Why would any company want to do this, you may ask? Because they feel that if you buy computer products from reader offers or subscribe to a certain type of publication, you are very likely to purchase their products too.

Cover mounts

Increasingly, demo versions of software are available on a CD/disk cover-mounted with the magazine. Sometimes you need to install the demo on your machine, or sometimes you can run it directly from the CD.

You can study all the features available from the demo (or cut-down) version of the software before making a decision to purchase.

Exhibitions

Most computer exhibitions tend to be open to trade customers and end users. Although, the organisers do reserve one or two days of the show for business and professional people only.

Computer exhibitions can be useful for fact-finding and for shopping. In the earlier days, most vendors used these shows for demonstration purposes only. Nowadays, to cover their costs of exhibiting, many vendors try to get direct sales at these shows. They will quite often offer their products at lower show prices to encourage customers to place their orders there and then. Several computer dealers also hire stands to sell leading products at low prices.

As a fact-finding venue, the major advantage of attending a computer exhibition is that you can see most branded products under one roof. There are staff present to demonstrate the products and answer any questions you may have. Be careful though, these demonstrators are sales people and may not be very generous in pointing out the limitations of their products. The other major advantage of attending computer exhibitions is that most vendors use these shows to launch new products. Regular visits to computer exhibitions will help you to keep up-to-date with the industry.

To choose your system, as well as knowing who the vendors are, you need to know their status in the industry. At computer shows, company status is very apparent. Companies with the clout in the industry get the most prominent positions – e.g. near the entrance. These companies also have big stands with large company logos. They go out of their way to build special stands with large screens, speakers and whatever else they can add to stand out from other companies. Smaller companies with limited budgets will have standard stands, in peripheral positions such as the sides and the back of the hall.

On entering a computer show, you may get a bit startled by the flashing lights and large, colourful screens everywhere. The way to ensure that your trip here is fruitful is to plan your day before you start. When you register at the entrance you will be offered a Show Guide. For some shows, you can get the show guides earlier by registering in advance. Use these guides to see who is exhibiting what and where. Plan your day carefully so that you can see all the products you want to and still have a couple of hours left to see anything new.

Computer dealers

In the early eighties, when the PC industry was in its infancy, computer dealers were very profitable. The computer industry was a fast-growing one and offering good profit margins. As a result, everyone and anyone wanted to get into the computing business. Anyone with a slight entrepreneurial flair wanted to jump on the bandwagon. Computer dealers were springing up everywhere – in high streets, local shopping areas and town outskirts. Even electrical retailers were turning into computer dealers! Sadly, most of these rising stars were not interested in computers. They were just keen to make lots of money. So here we are in the nineties, with more outlets selling computers than we need and not many computer dealers able to give us sound advice.

Before visiting a computer dealer, do your homework by reading the computer press. Also, learn and understand the basic terminology – a lot of it is explained in this book. Always remember that, if you want to pay the lowest price offered, you will usually not get the best support. To choose a good dealer, talk to friends or colleagues, and find out their experiences of your local dealer.

If there is a specific product you are interested in, call the vendor of that product first. Ask them who they recommend you buy their product from. They will always give you a reputable dealer contact in your area. Also ensure that the dealer is fully authorised to demonstrate and support the product.

Finally, since there are so many makes of computers and related products, most dealers cannot hold large stocks of any one item. Be prepared to place your order and wait a couple of days to pick it up.

High street stores

When low-price personal computers, from manufacturers such as Packard Bell in the UK, were introduced to the market, the general demand for personal computers was expected to boom. These expectations attracted retail chain stores such as Dixons to join the industry to sell low-end personal computers to consumers and small businesses.

The major attraction of buying your computer from one of these stores is the competitive prices they can offer. An independent dealer generally buys in small volumes and is given the standard trade discounts. High street chain stores can demand high discount from vendors because of their bulk buying nature. Hence, they can afford to pass on some of this discount to their customers.

The major drawback with these stores is that the shop assistants selling computers tend to be ex-television or ex-vacuum cleaner sales people. If you are lucky, you may be near a larger branch where they have a special "computer centre". Here they should be able to give you proper advice, although this cannot be guaranteed in all computer centres.

The other limitation with these stores is that they do not deal with all products. They only concentrate on products that are very popular.

To conclude, if you know what you want, and have a standard requirement, then you can take advantage of the low prices offered at these stores.

Computer superstores

This is the fastest growing sector in computer sales. The basic idea is to offer a wide range of hardware, software and accessories under one roof. Like the usual supermarkets, goods are stacked up on shelves and customers just go and pick what they want. To minimise rental costs and to offer a better shopping environment, these stores are located out of central shopping areas and offer ample car parking spaces.

Mail order

In the computer industry, mail order has become a popular way of shopping.

Firstly, there are the general mail order catalogue companies that offer a wide range of computer products including hardware, software and accessories. These companies have thick catalogues where they list all the products they carry. You can generally get good discounts and free carriage if your order value is substantial. When comparing prices do not forget to add carriage charges.

Some mail order companies offer free phone numbers for you to place your orders. Some also offer help lines for general advice. More reputable mail order companies even offer a free warranty against defects in workmanship.

Under the same general category fall computer dealers who also have a back-room mail order business. Some mail order dealers offer unbelievably low prices, especially on software. Check the versions of software they are offering. Quite often these packages are not genuine local versions, but are "grey-imports" from another country. Grey imports in the computer industry are products which are designed and priced to be used in the country of origin, but have been exported to another country, without the approval of vendors. American versions, for instance, are normally priced much lower than the UK versions. Hence, the UK dealer can afford to sell them at attractive prices. However, try and resist the temptation of buying these products – you will not get technical support from the vendors' local offices or favourably priced upgrades for your software.

The other type of mail order company is the product vendor who sells directly to the end customer by mail. With some vendors, such as Dell, you can buy their products directly. These manufacturers claim that by selling direct rather than through computer dealers they can offer lower prices. They can save the middleman's profits, and pass them on to you. They also claim that, this way they can have a direct relationship with their customers and provide better technical support. This is quite true with some of these companies. Dell's technical support, for instance, is rated quite highly in the industry. However, not all computer vendors selling direct can be rated so favourably.

Some mail order companies do not advertise but send details of their products or services directly to you by post. They usually obtain your details by renting a customer list from magazine publishers (as discussed under *Reader offers*) or other companies from whom you may have purchased something.

If you choose to buy your computer, software or other accessories by mail or telephone, it is wiser to use a credit card rather than sending a cheque. Should you have a dispute with the supplier, or should the company suddenly disappear and you have not received your goods, it may then be possible for you to get the credit card company to help you resolve the matter or provide you with a refund.

The other factor to look out for when buying by mail is whether the company offers a moneyback guarantee, should the product be unsuitable. You will usually find advertisements offering "30 Days Moneyback Guarantee".

When you have bought your new computer system check that all the parts are delivered and intact. Check that everything is working. If you have any problems, contact your supplier immediately.

Complete and send all the registration cards to the appropriate vendors straightaway. If you fail to register, you may have problems getting support. Also, with software, you will not qualify for upgrades at special prices, often offered to existing registered customers.

Internet

If you are the type that likes to shop from the comfort of a chair, then why not use the Internet! Obviously, you will need a computer connected to the Internet – if you have not yet bought your system, then you can try using someone else's or visit a *cybercafe* in your area and enjoy a cup of coffee at the same time.

Use indexes like Yahoo to find PC manufacturers, software vendors, etc. and browse through the latest products on their web sites. You may even be able to download some software directly via the Internet.

Windows

A computer is an extremely fast and efficient machine, but it is just that – a machine. It cannot think for itself and needs to be told exactly what to do. A simple operation, such as copying a file, involves the computer needing several instructions like find the file, read it, find empty space on the disk to write the new file, and so on. If you had to give your PC so many detailed commands every time you wanted to perform a simple operation, you would find it very cumbersome and time-consuming. You would probably give up using your PC altogether. In order to make life a little easier, an operating system exists to translate your intention to copy a file, and many other similar functions, into detailed instructions that control various components – like the disks, memory, monitor, and so on.

Windows, produced by the software giant Microsoft, is just such an operating system. It is known as a Graphical User Interface, *(or GUI, pronounced "gooey")*, since it uses graphical objects such as windows, icons and buttons – as opposed to the text-based input/output systems of older operating systems like DOS. It uses pictures, called *icons,* to represent programs and files. To start an application (such as an accounting or drawing program) in Windows, you either use your mouse to select its name and icon from a menu, or double-click on its desktop icon. For the beginner, the learning curve is reduced dramatically, since icons give clues to what programs you want to start, or what commands you want to issue. This is a very intuitive means of getting your computer to work for you, and doesn't require you to learn the many often abstract commands used by DOS. Since the Windows environment is very easy to use, it allows you to become productive very quickly in terms of using your applications.

The other factor that makes Windows so attractive is that software designed to run with it has a standard, consistent look and feel. The menus used by most applications have the same basic commands and structure, whether you're using a word-processor or a spreadsheet. For example if you have *File* as a menu heading, you can almost always expect to find functions like *Save* and *Exit* in the drop-down list. On the other hand, non-Windows software applications (though few are produced for the PC now) have different ways of performing basic functions, requiring you to spend time finding out the basic commands each time you use a new application.

Other major benefits that Windows offers are *Multitasking* and *Object Linking and Embedding* (OLE). Although at this stage you probably would not find much use for these facilities, you might as well be aware of what's on offer. Multitasking offers the Windows user the facility of running several programs at the same time. If you have to print a large document that takes quite a while to print, for instance, you can issue the print command from your word-processor to start the print job, leave it printing and open another window to start work on your spreadsheet.

OLE allows you to set up *hot-links* between common data in different software on your system. What this means in practice is that if you need to use the same data in more than one software application, you can set up a link so that each time you change the data in one application, the data in the other software will be updated automatically. For example, if you have a table in your spreadsheet which is also a part of a document in your word-processor, you can link the two so that every time you change the spreadsheet table, the word-processor document changes too.

The Windows desktop

The first thing you see once you turn on your computer and start Windows is the desktop, which should look something like the one shown below. Most of the screen is likely to be blank – this is the main desktop area, ready to be filled, if you wish, by *shortcut* icons for any of your applications. Along one edge of the screen (usually the bottom, though you can place it at whichever edge you

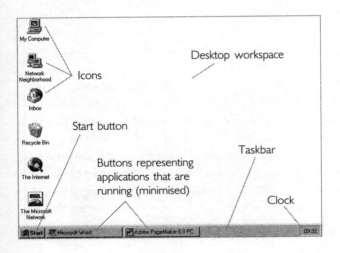

want) is the *taskbar*. One element is always present on the taskbar – the *Start button*. To start any program in Windows, you must begin by clicking on this button – unless you have set up a shortcut icon specifically for the purpose.

The taskbar may also contain a clock, and buttons representing applications that are already running: click on any of these to make that application the active window.

Starting programs

Any of the applications on your system can be started by clicking on the Start button, which is always present on the taskbar. You are presented with a menu, which should include, amongst others, the option *Programs*. If you rest your pointer over this, a sub-menu should appear,

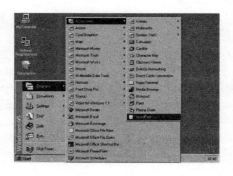

listing different programs and/or program groups (any menu item which has a black arrow to its right, and an icon representing a folder and a window to its left, indicates that a further sub-menu will appear if you rest your pointer over it). Continue in this way, navigating through the menu structure, until you see the name of the program you want to open (assuming that it has been installed properly). Click with your left mouse button on the name: the program will then start in a new window, and a button will appear for it on the taskbar.

Adding entries to the Start menu

To add an entry for a program or document to the Start menu, allowing you to start it easily without finding its file name in Windows Explorer or My Computer, use the following procedure. Choose Start>Settings>Taskbar, then click on the *Start Menu Programs* tab. Click on the Add button, then in the *Command Line:* dialog box enter the full pathname of the file, or click on Browse to find it from the directory structure. Click on Next, then double-click on the program folder in which you want the entry to appear. Give the program a suitable name in the dialog box that follows – this is what will appear on the Start menu. Click on Finish to add the entry to the Start menu.

Maximising, minimising and restoring windows

The window in which an application runs must be in one of three states: maximised, minimised or at an intermediate size. A maximised window occupies the whole of the screen, allowing you to see the greatest possible area of the document you are working on. A minimised window simply occupies a button on the taskbar; the application is still running, but its window's contents cannot be seen, and you cannot interact with it. A window of intermediate size is simply a cut-down version of a maximised window. It does not take up the whole of the screen, allowing you to see what is going on in any other applications you might have running. To adjust the size of a window, simply rest your pointer over one of the window's edges: the pointer should change to a double-headed arrow. Click with your left mouse button and drag the edge in or out until it's where you want it – then release the button.

When a window is in its maximised or intermediate state, you should see three buttons at the right of the title bar, which is the coloured band running across the top of the window. The Minimise button on the left looks like a minus-sign: click on this to reduce the application to a taskbar button. The Close button on the right looks like an "X": click here to finish this session with the program. Depending on the current state of the window, the central button will be either the Maximise (one rectangle) or Restore (two overlapping rectangles) button. Clicking on the Restore button will shrink the window from full-screen view to its previously set intermediate size.

The whole purpose of being able to run one or more windows in any of these different states is to allow you to take advantage of Windows' multitasking and OLE features (see above, in the introduction to this section). For example, if you are producing a financial report for your business, you might want to begin by running your accounting program (in a maximised window, to allow you to see as much as possible) to produce a pie chart of some aspect of the business's financial status. You might then minimise that window, and start your word-processor to write an introduction to the pie chart. Once you're happy with this, minimise the word-processor window and maximise the accounting program – then copy the pie chart to the Clipboard (see the appropriate part later in this section) and return to the word-processor. Paste the pie chart from the Clipboard into the document, below your introduction, and you have the first page of your report. Simple!

Windows Explorer and My Computer

While the procedure for starting an application that was explained in *Starting Programs* is valid for all programs on your system that have been properly installed, this does not mean that every program you have on your hard drive, floppy drive and CD-ROM can be started by selecting its name from the Start menu. An entry on the Start menu, or a shortcut icon on the desktop, is simply a quick and easy way of starting a program or opening a document: the Start menu is in no way supposed to be a comprehensive map of all the files on your system. Indeed, while the number of files accessible from the Start menu may be no more than perhaps 20, 30 or 40, you are likely to have thousands upon thousands of files on your system, stored on one medium or another. How do you know what's there?

One of the answers is to use Windows Explorer. This provides you with a means of examining the entire contents of all of your system by navigating your way through a map of the tree-like structure of media, folders, sub-folders and files. To start Windows Explorer, right-click on the Start button, then select *Explore* from the pop-up menu. You should see a window split into two panes. The pane on the left illustrates the hierarchical structure of the system, while the right-hand pane shows the contents of whatever folder or medium is selected on the left. For example, to navigate the contents of your hard drive, use the scroll bar at the right of the left-hand pane to move down the hierarchy until you see a grey box-like icon labelled with the letter that represents the hard disk (normally C:). Click on this, and the contents of the first hierarchical level of the drive will be displayed in the right-hand pane. This should consist of a number of folders, and perhaps some files. Folders are represented by an icon of a yellow loose-leaf folder, and may contain files or further sub-folders. Files, which may be programs, documents or elements used by those programs, have their own customised icons depending on what they are. To see the contents of a folder, double-click on it in the right-hand pane. To start a program, or to open a document, double-click on the appropriate icon.

Explorer is not just a tool to help you survey the catalogue of your files; you can also use it to move files to different locations, copy them and delete them.

To move a file from one location to another, or to copy it, click on it with your mouse to select it, then drag it over to the new location. Before releasing the mouse button, check the appearance of the pointer. If it appears as a normal arrow, then you are about to perform a Move operation; if it appears as an arrow with a plus-sign in a box near the arrow's tail, then you are about to Copy. The

initial state of the pointer depends on where you want to move/copy the file from and to. If the home and destination of the file are on the same drive, then the default operation will be a Move; if they are on different drives, then the default will be a Copy. Release the mouse button if the action you want to perform is indicated. Otherwise, press Ctrl to copy the file, or Shift to move it – then release the mouse button.

If you want to move or copy a group of files rather than a single one, press Ctrl while clicking on each file successively – then click on any of the highlighted files and drag as normal.

To delete a file, a group of files or a folder, select it, then press the Delete key.

Another way of examining the folders and files on your system is to use My Computer – double-click on the icon on the desktop. This fulfils a similar function to Windows Explorer, except that the display uses only one pane, giving perhaps a clearer and simpler view of a folder, but not allowing you to copy and move files so easily.

Icons and file extensions explained

Whenever you see a reference to one of your system's files, in Windows Explorer or My Computer, on the Start menu, and throughout Windows in general, it is represented not only by its name but also by an appropriate icon. For example, the word-processor program Word is represented by a particular icon, and all documents created under Word use the same icon. The potentially vast range of different icons that you are likely to encounter in the Windows environment may initially seem daunting, but it will soon become apparent that they are a very efficient means of immediately communicating the nature of the file they represent. They can certainly be used much more intuitively than the three-letter extensions that also accompany files (e.g., all Word document files have the file extension

.doc – so the full name of a Word file might be *letter.doc).*

File extensions are vital to your computer's handling of files, but are not always needed by the user, and by default are hidden in Windows. You can use Windows Explorer to display them: select *Options* from the *View* menu, and make sure the View tab is selected; then uncheck the box next to *Hide MS-DOS file extensions for file types that are registered*, and click OK.

One of the most important file extensions is *.exe*: this denotes an executable file, which is where the heart of any application resides. This is the file that is run whenever you start an application. Thus, if you used Windows Explorer to find a file called *winword.exe*, and double-clicked on it, then Word would start.

Another file extension you are likely to see is *.bak*, which is used by some programs to create a backup of the previously-saved version of the file you are using. When you save a file for the first time, it takes the file extension used as a default by the application. Then, when you save the file a second time, that first file is renamed with the extension *.bak*, and the new version again takes the application-specific extension. This way, if you realise that you have saved a file containing changes that you wish you hadn't made, you can always abandon the new version and revert to the backup.

Below is a selection of some of the most common icons, along with their file extensions (where appropriate) and meanings:

Word document file – .DOC

Open folder

Text file (use Notepad to read it) – .TXT

Closed folder

CorelDRAW! file – .COR

Floppy disk drive

DOS application file – .EXE

Hard drive (shared on a network)

Miscellaneous file (including .BAK)

The Clipboard

The Clipboard is not so much a program as an integral part of Windows. It is extremely versatile, and can be used, for example, simply to move some text around in a word-processor document, or, more ambitiously, to facilitate Object Linking and Embedding between two applications. It can be accessed from the Edit menu of most programs by using the commands Cut, Copy, Paste and Paste Special. The principle is simple: you either cut or copy a piece of text or an object (such as a picture, table or sound) to the Clipboard, then "paste" it in the desired position – which can be in the same document, or another document created by a different application. To copy to the Clipboard, select whatever you want to copy, then choose the Copy command from the Edit menu (or right-click with the mouse to bring up a similar, context-specific menu). The text or object is then copied to the Clipboard. To paste the contents of the Clipboard later on, simply choose Paste from the Edit menu. Anything you copy to the Clipboard will remain there until you subsequently replace it by copying something else, or until you switch off the computer.

Printing

A good deal of the tasks for which you use your computer will be meaningless unless you can print a "hard copy" of your work out onto paper. Printing in Windows is very easy: all applications that allow you to produce printable material will offer a Print command, normally under the File menu. You are then usually presented with a dialog box which allows you to select which pages of a document to print, how many pages, etc. Windows then does all the rest for you – you don't have to configure each individual application to use your printer, since all applications use the same settings with which you initially provide

Windows. To add a printer, or to modify the settings that apply to a printer already installed, select Start>Settings>Printers, then double-click on the appropriate icon in the Printers window.

Another benefit of using a common printer driver for all Windows applications is that you can use any of the fonts installed on your system in any of your applications. To see a list of all the fonts currently available to you, choose Start>Settings>Control Panel, then double-click on the Fonts shortcut icon – or open the c:\windows\fonts folder.

One very easy way of printing a file is to drag the file's icon onto your printer's icon. This can be found in the

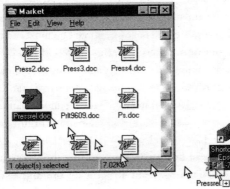

window summoned by selecting Start>Settings>Printers; alternatively, you may wish to set up a shortcut icon for the printer, on your desktop. To do this, click on the icon in the Printers window and drag it out onto the desktop using the right mouse button, then select *Create Shortcut(s) here* from the context menu that pops up. Now, all you have to do to print a single copy of the full document is drag its icon out of Windows Explorer, or a My Computer window, and onto this desktop shortcut icon.

Formatting a floppy disk

While a hard drive can hold a huge amount of information, probably over 1,000 times as much as a floppy disk, there is likely to come a time when you need to transfer information from your hard drive to another computer, or to back up some files for safe keeping. The most common method of doing either of these tasks – if you're not connected to a network and don't have an expensive writable CD-ROM drive – is to use floppy disks. These are a cheap and effective means of storing and transporting small amounts of data, a normal 3½ inch high-density disk holding 1.44 megabytes.

Before you can do anything with a floppy disk, it must be formatted. This involves structuring the disk using a system of tracks and sectors, in order to allow your computer to store and locate data on it. Many floppy disks nowadays are sold preformatted, but it is still often a little cheaper to buy non-formatted disks and format them yourself. To do this, first insert the disk you want to format (or reformat) into your floppy disk drive. Now open Windows Explorer or My Computer, and right-click on the floppy disk icon. A context menu should appear, offering the command *Format...* Click this to call the Format dialog box, which offers you various options concerning the nature of the format. Enter a label for the disk (this is optional, though it will allow you to identify it easily in future if the sticky label falls off or becomes illegible), then click Start. Windows will now take a minute or two to format your disk.

Customising Windows

By default, Windows has a functional but very dull appearance, using grey windows, grey buttons, a grey taskbar and an ocean-green desktop. If you have a sound card, then when certain system events occur, Windows will use exactly the same Microsoft-standard bleeps and chimes that are heard by millions of other users world-wide. You can change all of this. If you want, you can have orange-bordered windows with bright-green buttons and a purple workspace. You can cover your desktop with any image you want, and have Windows bark at you when you hit the wrong key.

There are many ways in which the appearance and functioning of the desktop can be customised. To make any changes, click anywhere on the desktop with your right mouse button to call Display Properties. You will see a window with at least four tabs:

- *Background* allows you to change the appearance of the area that is seen behind the taskbar and any windows you might have open. You can cover the area either with a simple pattern, or with a wallpaper, which may be anything from a small tile pattern to a full-screen picture. Click on the name of a background that you think looks interesting, and see how it will look in the example screen at the centre of the window. If you have somewhere on your system a bitmap image, such as a digitised photograph, that you would like to use for your wallpaper, click on the Browse button and select the file. When you're satisfied, click *Apply* to cover the actual background of your desktop.

- *Screen Saver* lets you change the animated screen that temporarily replaces your desktop when you haven't touched your mouse or keyboard for a while

– this helps protect your monitor from screen-burn, which is when an image that has been displayed for a long time is "burnt" into the screen, leaving a shadow of the image even after the actual display has updated. Select any of the installed screensavers from the drop-down menu, then click apply. Again, a preview is displayed in the example screen at the centre of the window.

- *Appearance* lets you change the way windows look. For example, you can alter the colour of your windows' borders and workspace, and the font used by window headings and menus.

- *Settings* allows you to modify the colour and resolution settings used for the display of Windows.

If you have a sound card and want to change the sounds assigned to Windows system events, double-click on My Computer, then on the Control Panel icon, and finally the Sounds icon. At the top of the Sounds tab, under the heading "Events:", is a scrollable list of all the system events that Windows recognises – things like starting or exiting Windows, or the error that occurs when you try to scroll beyond the end of a word-processor document. A "speaker" icon appears to the left of every system event that has a sound assigned to it. Below this, under the heading "Name:", is a list of wave sound files: any of these may be linked to a system event. If a sound file that you know is on your system somewhere is not displayed in this list, click on Browse to select it. Go through the Events list, assigning whatever sounds you want, then click OK.

The DOS prompt

Before the advent of Windows, DOS was the underlying operating system for almost all PCs. Early versions of Windows operated "on top of" DOS, providing a user-friendly way of communicating with DOS, but not strictly functioning as the base operating system. When a computer with Windows 3.1 was turned on, DOS was loaded initially, and then, if the user so wished, Windows could be loaded. Many programs were written to be used under DOS, not Windows, and while these could usually be accessed through Windows, via a pseudo-DOS prompt, the slow speed at which they often ran made it more practical to exit Windows completely and run them from true DOS.

Windows 95 changed all of this. DOS is no longer needed to run in the background; Windows loads directly, as soon as you turn on your computer. More and more programs now are designed to use the intuitive Windows user interface, rather than DOS, which is becoming increasingly obsolete for the average user.

However, many users of Windows are likely still to have some old DOS programs on their system, and may still need to access them, perhaps because they need to access data entered with these programs that they have not been able to convert to some Windows-compatible format.

To access the DOS prompt, choose Start>Programs>MS-DOS Prompt. The window that appears has an icon bar along its top edge, incorporating icons that allow you, for example, to change the appearance of the DOS interface, and to copy and paste between DOS and Windows applications. To start a program from the DOS prompt, enter its pathname, or navigate through the directory structure using the appropriate commands, such as *cd [directory]*, and enter the name of the *.exe* file – then press Return. For information on any of the DOS commands, enter the command followed by */?* – e.g., *cd /?* – and press Return.

To run an MS-DOS program, you don't need to enter its pathname from the DOS prompt: you can simply click on its file from Windows Explorer or My Computer – or even give it a shortcut icon, or an entry on the Start menu.

To exit from an MS-DOS window, type exit and hit

Return, or simply click on the Close button (X) in the
DOS window's top right-hand corner.

Windows housekeeping

Just as with the household chores of dusting, emptying
the bins and doing the laundry, there are some tasks that
need to be done by anyone who spends part of their time
living in a Windows environment. These are often boring,
unwanted interruptions to your agenda, but you'll feel
better after you've done them, and in the future you'll
thank yourself for being so diligent. The main Windows
housekeeping tasks are performing backups and cleaning
out unwanted files.

Backups

One day in the future, you'll turn on your computer,
listen to your computer making an ugly, unusual whirring
noise, and then discover that your hard drive has decided
not to work, and won't boot up, locking all your precious
data inside it with no way of getting at it. Alternatively,
your PC might become infected by a virus that destroys
some or all of your data; or you might simply erase it
yourself by accident. In any of these situations, a backup
will not solve your problem, but will make your life a
great deal easier once you've got it fixed.

A backup is a copy of some or all of the files on your hard drive, usually stored on floppy disk. The files are compressed, so as to reduce the number of floppy disks you need to use. If you need to retrieve the files from the backup disks, it is a simple task to restore the files to your hard drive – the backup program will even remember where the files came from, and put them back in their original folders. Windows comes with such a program, which you can find by selecting Programs> Accessories>System Tools>Backup from the Start menu.

The first thing you see on running Backup, once you have got rid of the introductory screens, is a window with an interface that looks a lot like Windows Explorer. The window has three tabs: *Backup*, *Restore* and *Compare*. The first creates backup files and saves them to your storage medium; the second restores them to your hard drive; and the third lets you compare the contents of a backup with any number of hard-drive files you select.

The process of backing up is very simple; the program virtually holds your hand as you tell it the details it needs to know. With the *Backup* tab selected, the first step is to select which files you want to back up. You navigate through the folders just as you would with Windows Explorer, by clicking on folders in the left-hand pane (or double-clicking on folders in the right-hand pane). The main difference between the Explorer and the Backup interface is that every drive, folder and file has an empty square box to its left. To select any element for backup, you simply put a tick in its box – you can do this by left-clicking on the box. The Status bar at the bottom of the Backup window will tell you how many files you have selected, and how many kilobytes these files take up.

When you've selected all the files you want to back up, click on the Next Step button at the top-right of the window. You are now prompted to specify where you want to store your backup. This will probably be a floppy disk drive, but you may have a backup drive, devised specifically for fast, efficient backups, or a recordable CD drive. If you are using floppies, place a blank disk in the drive now. Select the device by clicking on it, then click the *Start Backup* button to continue. If your backup is to take up more than one floppy disk, you will be prompted to insert new disks as they are needed.

The compression system used by the Backup program will drastically reduce the number of disks you need to use. The exact degree of compression will depend on the types of files you are backing up. Text files will compress the most; graphics files may already be saved in some compressed form, and so it may not be possible to reduce their size very much more.

If you are short of hard-drive space, but find that you use most of the files you have on it and don't want to spend time moving files to and from floppy disks, you could always back up some files to the same hard drive, using the compression to shrink them down, and then erase the original files. It would then be a very simple matter to restore the compressed files to their former state – and the process would be very quick, since the access time of the hard drive is very much shorter than that of the floppy drive.

Windows backups are also a very useful way of exchanging large files, or groups of files, with friends or colleagues. You don't have to restore a backup to the computer from which it was taken: anyone else can easily restore it to any directory of their PC, as long as they have the same version of the same backup program that you use. An archiving/compression utility like Windows Backup is absolutely necessary if you wish to use floppy disks to exchange files that are longer than 1.44Mb – otherwise the files won't fit on one disk, and there is no other way of breaking them up into manageable pieces. PKZIP is the most popular compression program for the PC, and offers very efficient compression levels, but the tremendous ease of use offered by Windows Backup, and the fact that it is owned by everyone with Windows, may mean that fewer and fewer people find the need to use a dedicated compression program like PKZIP, when Backup can do most of the same things just as well.

Restoring or comparing backup files is just as simple, using the same methods to select the files you want to work with. Again, the program prompts you for all the information it needs, so this doesn't require any step-by-step analysis here. Beware, however, of trying to use Windows 95 Backup or above to restore backups made with earlier versions (such as that shipped with Windows 3.1): it won't work. You might expect the new version of Backup to be backwards-compatible (how else are you to restore backups made years ago on the old operating system, unless you have still kept access to the old Backup routines?), but it seems that improvements in the software made compatibility impossible.

How often you back up the files on your computer should depend on how often you use it, and on how much you revise the files every session. If you only use your computer once a week to play a quick game of Lemmings, you might feel confident in performing a backup once every month. If, on the other hand, you use your computer at work every day to maintain a customer database which is growing constantly, it is advisable that you back up your data daily.

The most common way of performing regular backups is to use the "Grandfather, father, son" method. As the name implies, this uses three generations of backup storage media. Let's say you perform a backup of your customer database every day, and that each backup can fit on one floppy disk. On Monday, you back up your files to a first-generation disk. On Tuesday, you use a new disk – this becomes the "son", and Monday's is now the "father". On Wednesday, the third new disk becomes the latest "son", and the disks used on the previous two days augment by a generation. When you get to Thursday, you've used up all your disks. So you take yesterday's "grandfather", the disk you first used on Monday, and make that today's son. Thus, the three disks continue to "leapfrog" each other. The advantage of this system over simply backing up to the same disk every day is that you always have three different records of your files at different stages of development. If you realise that yesterday you made unwanted changes that were saved to your current "father" disk, you can always restore the backup from the "grandfather". Also, if your floppy disk drive chews up today's "son", you have two copies to fall back on. Many people additionally make a separate backup, e.g. once every week, which ensures in the case of a problem not immediately detected that you always have a copy of your files that is more than two or three days old.

Clearing out unwanted files

The hard drive on your PC is likely to hold thousands upon thousands of files, many of which you'll never know about, and many others whose function you are unsure of. It is also likely that, as you add new files to your PC, creating new documents, installing new programs and removing old ones, some files will be left that are completely redundant. There is no reason for such files to carry on clogging up your hard drive, and getting rid of them might free up a surprising amount of space. The problem, of course, is knowing which files are useless, and which are essential to the operating system or your various, expensive applications. You might be tempted therefore to leave them alone. However, there is a lot you can do without worrying about crippling Windows or your favourite programs, just as long as you take precautions. And if in doubt, don't touch it.

Firstly, it should be said that there are many excellent file management utilities and uninstallers which will do some of these jobs for you. Uninstallers, for instance, record exactly which files are added to your hard drive when you install an application. If later you decide that you don't want to continue using that application, you simply tell your uninstaller which one you wish to remove, and it will erase from your hard drive not only the main executable file, but all the other peripheral files (often hundreds) that enable it to function – no matter how many different folders the files are located in. Windows comes with a utility that enables you to remove an application and all of its related files in one fell swoop. To access this, select Settings>Control Panel from the Start menu, then double-click on the *Add/Remove Programs* icon. However, it can only handle programs that were designed to take advantage of special Windows features like this. This should not be a problem with newer programs, but to uninstall anything created before the arrival of Windows 95 you'll need to use another method. Before you begin tentatively to remove files with Windows Explorer, check that within the application's program group there isn't an icon labelled something like "Uninstall": some applications come with their own program-specific uninstaller utilities.

You may not have an uninstaller, though; and even if you do, there are some functions (such as deciding which word-processor documents are no longer of any use to you) which it cannot perform. You may then be able to rid yourself of some redundant files by any of the following methods:

The Recycle Bin

Whenever you "delete" a file in Windows, which you would normally do by using Windows Explorer, it is not immediately removed from your drive, but sent to the Recycle Bin. This feature is designed to act as a safeguard in the event of your accidentally deleting files. Hence, when you delete a file, you do not actually gain any extra space on your drive until you remove the item from your Recycle Bin. To view its contents, double-click on the Recycle Bin icon, which you should find on your desktop. A list of all the files residing there will be displayed in a format similar to that of the right-hand pane of the Windows Explorer. To remove files from the Recycle Bin, select them using the Control key and the left mouse button, then choose Delete from the File menu – or simply hit the *Delete* key. Once you confirm that you do actually want to go through with this action, the file will be removed and you will no longer be able to retrieve it. Alternatively, to purge its whole contents, select Empty Recycle Bin from the File menu.

If you decide that you want to rescue a file from the Recycle Bin, select it, then choose Restore from the File menu. It will then be returned to its original location.

Old data files

The first step is to assess all of the document-type files

that you have created, and delete and/or back up any that you don't need. The locations of these files will depend on what application they belong to. For example, Microsoft Word usually stores its documents in a folder named *C:\My Documents*, while the data for most other applications are stored in a sub-folder of the one that holds everything related to that application, including the main program files. If you can decide which files are no longer needed by looking at the titles you have given them, it's probably easiest to delete them with Windows Explorer; otherwise, it's probably best to examine the files using the relevant applications. Let us say that you have opened Word to examine an old document, and have decided that you no longer need it. First, close the document. You could use Windows Explorer to delete it, but many programs compatible with Windows offer a quicker method: simply open any of the file dialog boxes (such as the *Open* dialog), then right-click on the file and select *Delete* from the pop-up menu.

Program-specific backup files

Remove any backup files specific to particular applications. For example, several programs, including CorelDRAW!, keep a copy not only of the current version of a data file, but also of the previous version, renaming it **.bak*. These are often a handy safety net, protecting you against unwanted changes or accidental deletions, but the files may often be very large. If you find a large file with an accompanying *.bak* file, neither of which have been amended recently, it's probably best to delete the backup.

Remember, these backup files are *not* related to the files created with the Backup utility described earlier.

*.tmp files

Remove the *.tmp* (short for "temporary") files that are lurking on your hard drive. These are files created by Windows, usually as temporary backups, while it is in the process of performing certain tasks. If something were to go wrong in a procedure, you could revert to this backup. Normally, Windows erases these files automatically after they are no longer needed. However, if something goes wrong – e.g., your computer might hang, requiring you to reboot – a *.tmp* file might remain on the hard drive, even though it may no longer be of any use to you. If you were forced to quit an application prematurely without saving the document you were working on, or if you had to reboot, then it might be possible to restore the file you thought you had lost from one of these *.tmp* files – if you can work out which is the file you need. For example, PageMaker creates *.tmp* files with names like *Pm6f361.tmp*. Otherwise, you may need to do a little detective work: this is one good reason for clearing the rubbish out of your *temp* directory regularly.

Under your *Windows* folder, you should see a folder named *Temp*. This is where Windows stores its **.tmp* files, with names like *~df1324.tmp*. Windows Explorer will show you that many of the files have a size of "0K", and thus hold no information; others could be several megabytes long. If you haven't had any recent system or application failures, and haven't seemingly lost any important files, then it's quite safe to delete any **.tmp* files you find. Before doing so, it's safest to make sure you have no other applications (which might currently be using **.tmp* files) open except for Windows Explorer or My Computer. Select the files to delete using the methods given in the *Windows Explorer and My Computer* topic earlier – then hit the Delete key, and confirm the action. Remember, if you are using the Recycle Bin, these files will have to be cleared out of the bin before they are truly removed from your hard drive.

Removing applications without an uninstaller

If you don't have an uninstaller, or if the one you do have is not compatible with an application you want to remove, then you can always remove files manually, as long as you're careful. (Remember, removing an application from your Start menu simply deletes the "signpost" that Windows offers you to allow you to start the application without selecting its *.exe* file from Explorer. If you only do this, the files that comprise the program still remain on your hard drive.) If you are going to remove an application, you need to know which folder on your hard drive it is located in. If the application has a Start menu entry, you can easily find where the folder is. Right-click on the Start menu, then select *Explore*. Now open up the folder *C:\Windows\Start Menu\Programs*. The structure of the files and sub-folders beneath this folder should be familiar to you, since this is the "map" that Windows uses to generate the structure of the Start menu. The program icons you see here do not represent the programs themselves (they all have a size of only 1K), but are merely shortcuts to those programs. Navigate your way through the tree of folders until you come to the entry for the file you want to delete (look for the icon that accompanies its entry on the Start menu). Now right-click on its icon and select *Properties* from the pop-up menu. If you have selected the correct file, there should be a *Shortcut* tab in the Window which appears. Select this. In the box labelled *Target*, you will see a pathname: this is the location of the program file on your hard drive. Make a note of this, cancel out of the Properties box, and navigate to the program's folder. The application's main folder may structure its contents using sub-folders, but somewhere within it you should find at least one application file, a help file and some data files. (There are likely to be others, such as text files explaining how to install the application, how to upgrade, etc.) As long as you are absolutely sure you no longer want this application, it should be safe to delete its main folder and everything below it; any files belonging to other applications are there because of poor organisation. Again, it should be stressed: if in doubt, leave the files alone.

Defragmenting

When a hard disk or floppy disk is formatted, it is organised into different areas, each with its own address, which enable the disk controller software to find the position on the disk where it wants to read or record data. When a file is written to disk, the controller software tries to keep all of the file in the same location, so that it will be easy to read back all of the file in one go; but if the file is too large to fit into a single available location, it will be split up and distributed around different areas of the disk, the different sections of data being linked to each other by pointers. This happens increasingly as revised files grow, and as old files are deleted, leaving gaps which must be filled up. The problem with the fragmenting of files is that it results in an extended disk access time, as the drive has to make a new search for each separate part of a file.

Windows comes with a program called Disk Defragmenter, which reorganises the data on your disk so that files are stored in contiguous areas – meaning that only one fresh search is needed for each file that needs to be read or written. To run the program, select Programs>Accessories>System Tools>Disk Defragmenter from the Start Menu. Now select the drive that you wish to defragment, and click *OK*. The program will first analyse the contents of the selected drive, and suggest whether it is worth defragmenting it. Whatever its suggestion, you can decide whether to defragment or cancel out of the program. If you continue, you are presented with a schematic representation of the different

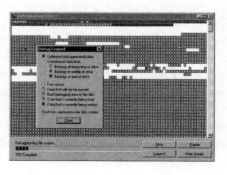

clusters of data on your drive, which you can see being rearranged as Disk Defragmenter does its job. A hard drive usually takes around half an hour to defragment, though the time will depend on the speed and size of the drive, and the speed of your computer.

ScanDisk

This is another program that is provided with Windows, and is used to check that a floppy or hard disk is in good working order. Both the disk's physical integrity and the organisation of the data on it are checked, and it is often possible to make repairs if any problems are found.

To run ScanDisk, select Programs>Accessories>System Tools from the Start menu. You then need to specify which drive to check, and whether you want to examine just the data, or both the data and the physical surface of the disk. When you click *Start*, you are presented with an interface similar to that of Disk Defragmenter, representing each of the clusters of data. One problem that may occur with the data is that the pointers linking fragmented clusters could contain incorrect references. This often means that the badly referenced data is lost, but it is sometimes possible for ScanDisk to recover at least some of the corrupted file. Another possible problem, and one that is rather more serious, is that the magnetic surface of the disk may be damaged. This is more common with floppy disks than with hard drives, since floppies are more exposed to dust and the elements. Such a problem does not mean that the whole of your data is corrupted; indeed, if only a few disk clusters are damaged, and if your disk hasn't needed to access those clusters, you won't even be aware of the problem. When ScanDisk detects a damaged sector, it can mark that sector as "bad": no attempt will then be made to write to that sector in the future.

Networking

Another important facility available in Windows is networking, which allows you to communicate with other computers, either on a local network of computers connected via network cards and cables, or, using "dial-up networking", via modems connected to the telephone system. All the resources of the networked computers can then be shared. This means that you can access and amend a document file, for instance, that is located on the hard drive of another computer, and then print the finished document to a printer connected to yet another computer. The remote computer(s) could be in the office next to yours, or on the other side of the world. If your computer is connected to a network and correctly set up, a Network Neighborhood icon should appear on your desktop. Double-clicking on this allows access to all the

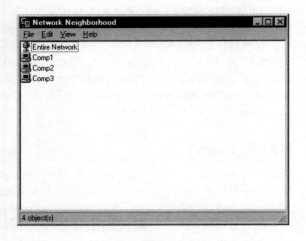

computers on your network, using the directory tree structure you will by now be familiar with.

The Internet

"Internet", "World-Wide Web", "Information Superhighway", "Cyberspace", "Intranet", "Global Village": you are barely able to pick up a newspaper or turn on the television nowadays without having these terms dangled tantalisingly in front of you. Rarely, though, do the media pause to explain what they actually mean. Everyone has at least some vague notion that they all involve computers somehow talking to each other, but it can be surprisingly hard for an outsider to progress beyond this rudimentary knowledge.

What, then, is the Internet? Basically, it is a network of computers all around the world that are linked together, normally via telephone lines, in order to be able to exchange information with each other. Academic institutions, commercial organisations, the military and private individuals alike may use the same network for their own particular ends. Depending on who you are, you can use the Internet to exchange research data with a colleague at another university, seal a business deal, learn whom you're supposed to be bombing today, or get the most up-to-date weather report for your area. So how is this possible, and why did it all start?

A brief history

In the middle of the Cold War, America's military bigwigs, feeling the threat of nuclear hostility from the USSR, decided that they had a problem on their hands: how would they be able to communicate with each other during and after a nuclear attack? Some of the telephone lines might be down, radio stations could be inoperable, and anyone risking their health to come above ground might find roads blocked. It was not enough, for example, simply to bury the telephone lines deeper, for those telephone lines, and the control centres connecting them, would be obvious targets for attack. Therefore, it was decided that any effective communications system had to have no particular centre, and no absolutely vital pathways connecting the various military bases. Thus, if base B were attacked, bases A and C should be able to talk to each other without worrying that one of their possible connection points had been destroyed. A true network, then, was needed – one comprised of a number of bases, each of equal status, and each with a number of potential ways of connecting to any other.

Though proposed by the US in 1964, the first example of such a network was developed in the UK, at the National Physical Laboratory in 1968. This, however, did not begin to approach the size or complexity of the system envisaged by the Pentagon, which the following year, through its Advanced Research Projects Agency, gave birth to ARPANET. Developed by scientists, this was essentially a network of a handful of computers at educational sites which facilitated the transfer of scientific research data. By 1972, ARPANET linked 37 sites. The network continued to grow, until in 1983 it spawned a military branch, MILNET, which allowed more rigorous security to be maintained. 1984 saw the arrival of a further network, NSFNET, the National Science Foundation Network, which used newer, faster computers and allowed users at any academic establishment to access its data. In the UK, computers at five universities were linked in the late 1970s. More universities joined the network, until it grew into JANET, the Joint Academic Network.

In the 1980s all of these networks, along with similar systems in other countries, began to join together to form an international network of networks. Thus the Internet was born, and began to grow exponentially as more and more organisations and individuals took advantage of this global means of communicating.

At this point, some researchers at CERN, the European Centre for Nuclear Research, realised that while the Internet offered an unparalleled communication medium, the various methods of communication differed according to what sort of information one wanted to access, and where one was accessing it from. A new, uniform environment was needed, which would allow anyone, anywhere, sitting at any popular type of computer terminal to access any sort of Internet information using a single interface. These researchers developed the World-Wide Web, a medium using electronic "pages" of text and images that resembled the format of a magazine, which could be linked together where relevant.

Service providers

Some large establishments, such as universities, have a direct connection to the Internet. This means that they are permanently linked. Anyone using the Internet from such a site does not have to worry about modems, communications protocols or telephone bills: everything is already set up and paid for. However, the individual who wishes to use the Internet from the home or the office will need to do so via a *service provider*. The service provider is directly connected to the Internet, as a university would be: the individual dials in to the service provider via the telephone system, and gains indirect access to the Internet, paying the service provider for the privilege. In order to connect your computer to the Internet, you need a *modem*, which translates the computer's binary electrical signal into audible beeps and whirrs that can be sent along the telephone line.

At the service provider's end of the telephone line are many modems, which will link you to the Internet, either fully or to a limited extent, and may also let you access some facilities offered by the provider for the exclusive use of its customers. This is where the distinction lies between the two basic types of service providers. The older type of provider is essentially an overgrown bulletin board. Originally, these allowed the user to exchange messages with other members of the same bulletin board, access repositories of information and software stored there, and little else. Because of the current popularity of the Internet, the major ex-bulletin board service providers now offer Internet access – CompuServe, for instance, now offers full Internet access.

Nowadays, however, virtually anything you can get from a bulletin board (except perhaps the cosy atmosphere) can also be had from the Internet, only on a larger scale, and with much more variety. For this reason, most new service providers, like the older Demon and Pipex, offer only an Internet connection, with few additional services. They generally charge a flat rate for connection, either monthly or annually, so your service provider's bill will not change whether you spend five minutes or fifty hours a week on the Internet.

However, there is one other, very important factor governing the cost – and hence the length – of your connection: the telephone bill. This is likely to be what eats up most of the money you spend on the Internet. Most service providers offer "nodes" in your area, which allow you to connect to them for the cost of a local telephone call. This may mean that calls are charged at a fairly cheap rate, especially at the weekend – but the Internet, especially the World-Wide Web, can be very addictive, and it is not unusual for an Internet connection to last two hours or more. Add to this the fact that you may want to log on several times a week, to check your e-mail in-box, for instance, or to catch up on the latest in your Usenet newsgroups, and you could find that your quarterly phone bill is twice (or more) what it was before you bought a modem.

When choosing a service provider, you shouldn't only take into account things like the monthly rate, or charges for extra services. One other very important factor is the ratio of modems to users, and the speed at which these modems run. For instance, it is common for a service provider to have one modem for every 30 of its customers. Such a ratio is likely to mean that you would be able to connect immediately during the daytime of most weekdays; but if you try calling on a Saturday evening, for instance, when many users are at home and the rates are cheap, you may often find that there are no free modems at the provider's end to take your call. At such times also, the speed of the network may slow down to a crawl, as it is burdened with the task of dealing with several thousand users at a time. And no matter how many people you're sharing the network with, your connection will be no faster than the slower of the two modems involved. So, despite how proud you are of your shiny new 33.6 kbps (kilobytes per second, the rate of data transfer) modem, if you're connected to a service provider modem that runs at 28.8 kbps, then that's the speed at which your connection will run. You are then likely to spend longer than you would wish in performing any specific task on the Internet, and your telephone bill for that session will consequently be higher. However, most service providers are likely to eventually upgrade their modems to the latest fast modems introduced to the market.

ISDN

As has been said already, most Internet connections are made using the existing network of telephone lines. One major drawback of this is that telephone lines were designed to carry an analogue electrical signal suitable only for the transmission of sound. This means that the digital signal used by computers has to be converted into sound, transmitted electrically, then converted back into a digital signal for processing by a computer at the other end of the line. The *bandwidth*, or frequency range, used by telephone lines is perfectly adequate for voice transmission, but not suitable for digital data, which could be transmitted faster and more efficiently using a wider bandwidth. In the past, the *bottleneck* (the single element that most restricts the speed of transmission) in long-distance computer communications was the speed of the modem. Now that modem speeds have improved dramatically, the bottleneck is coming to be the telephone line, since the wide bandwidth which would most suit the computer signal is not catered for. One solution to this problem is ISDN, or *Integrated Services Digital Network*. This uses fibre-optic cables to enable direct digital transmission of data using the full bandwidth, meaning that it is not necessary to convert the signal from digital to analogue, and back to digital again *(see Modem, Section 1: The PC Unravelled)*. This would make it possible to receive data from a remote computer almost as quickly as from one's own hard drive. ISDN has not yet gained very large public popularity, but if we are actually to have the "digital revolution" that we hear so much speculation about, with its interactive multimedia services and video-conferencing, then some means of digital communication, like ISDN, is needed.

Internet software

Once you have a computer, a telephone line, a service provider and a modem, all you need is some software to enable you to tell your modem what to do and where to do it. This software falls into two basic categories. First you need some connection software that will allow your computer to talk to your service provider's; and then you need some Internet application software to allow you to interface easily with the different types of information sources you will find.

All computers on the Internet communicate with each other through a common digital language, or set of standards, known as TCP/IP (this stands for *Transmission Control Protocol/Internet Protocol*). The connection software used by your computer is called a *winsock*, and uses TCP/IP to control how your computer communicates with your modem, and how your modem communicates with your service provider's modem. This may require you to enter some settings before you log on to your service provider for the first time, but once these are established you shouldn't have to worry about them again. Windows comes with a built-in winsock, but if you have an earlier version of Windows, or prefer to use other software anyway, then your service provider should provide you with the necessary communications software on disk. (The most popular alternative is a shareware program called Trumpet Winsock, whose latest version can be downloaded from Trumpet's Web site at www.trumpet.com.au.) The connection software may also store customer information about you, such as your account details and password, and will automatically submit these to the host computer every time you log on. Instructions about how to configure your connection software should be included in the starter pack you receive from your service provider on opening an account.

To connect to the Internet, then, you need to run your winsock software, minimise its window, then run your Internet application software. What this is will depend on what sort of Internet resource you intend to access. The main areas of the Internet, and the software needed to visit them, are discussed below.

The World-Wide Web (WWW)

The first thing you are likely to want to do on the Internet – and the easiest – is to surf the World-Wide Web. Other, older means of accessing information on the Internet often required the user to learn many specific commands necessary for, say, navigating through archives of computer files and downloading them, and were largely text-based. Browsing the Web, however, is a lot like leafing through a huge, glossy magazine, only one with sound, film and animation.

Another major feature of the web is the presence of *hot-links,* which again are a great improvement on previous Internet environments. Anyone without Web access who wants to glean any information from the Internet has to know more or less precisely where they want to go and what they want to do there. For example, let us say I want to download a copy of the complete text of Shakespeare's *The Tempest* from an FTP site whose address has been given in a computer magazine. This is simple enough: I simply enter the full address, down to the title of the file I want, into the location box of my FTP client, exactly as it is printed in the magazine. However, on the same server, in another directory, there might be a file containing a useful piece of literary criticism on *The Tempest*, which I would have no way of knowing about without searching through that directory. There might also be similarly relevant files on other servers located elsewhere, about which I would be equally ignorant. This makes the process of performing FTP transactions very linear and often very laborious.

The Web's hot-links, however, do away with this problem. Imagine reading a magazine article with an extensive bibliography containing references to many other related sources, in other magazines, books, essays, even films. Now imagine that every reference, instead of being numbered and listed at the end of the article, was simply underlined, and that you could summon up any one of those sources simply by pointing with your finger at any of the underlined references. Such a situation is clearly physically impossible, but it is very much akin to what browsing the Web is like. Almost every Web article, or *page*, has several hot-links, indicated by underlined text or labelled graphics, which you simply point at with your mouse and click, in order to move to a related page. This page can be located at the same Web site in the same building as the current one, or halfway around the world.

Thus, for example, a Web site located in Chicago which holds archives of classical music might contain a link to a site in Vienna containing information on a particular composer. A user would be able to jump from one site to another at the click of a button, without having to go through the rigmarole of leaving the first site, finding the address of the second, and then manually making a new connection.

Web browsers

The tool, or interface, needed to access web sites is known as a "web browser", and uses a system of codes known as *HyperText Markup Language* (HTML – see the topic *HTML and Web page design*) to provide these links and visual effects. The major browsers today are *Netscape Navigator* and *Microsoft Internet Explorer*. (The other sorts of software you might need for various other Internet activities are covered later, in the appropriate topics.)

Netscape Navigator

Navigator is the name of Netscape's WWW browser, though its huge popularity eclipses that of other earlier Netscape products so much that it is often known simply as Netscape. When you sign up with a service provider, you will be given some software to enable you to connect easily with them. This will include a Web browser, though it is unlikely to be Netscape Navigator. If you want a copy, use the browser you do have to connect to Netscape's web site at www.netscape.com, and download it from there. You can initially do so for free, but if after you have evaluated it you feel that you are likely to continue to use it, you are expected to buy a licence for a fee.

Microsoft Internet Explorer

While Navigator has been the most popular Web browser around, with over 80% of market share, the challenge by Microsoft with its new version of Internet Explorer may change all that. Navigator offers many advanced features, making it a very comprehensive browser, but this means that the program is fairly cumbersome: it takes up a significant amount of space on your hard drive, and often runs a little slowly. Internet Explorer is smaller and faster, and what's more, it's currently completely free. While most of Navigator's users are probably still "evaluating", having paid nothing to Netscape, the fact that you can use Internet Explorer for free with a clear conscience may do a lot – along with Microsoft's huge clout in the industry – to help it gain ground on the competition. Internet Explorer can be downloaded from Microsoft's Web site at www.microsoft.com/ie.

Microsoft has also introduced an innovative addition to its Internet technology: the concept of *ActiveX*. This promises to facilitate the development of an Internet environment using improved animation, 3-D virtual reality and enhanced multimedia capabilities. ActiveX is being used to incorporate Internet capabilities directly into the Windows operating system, so that the Internet can be accessed directly, without having to use a Web browser, say, as mediator. On this principle, it should be as easy to access a file on some remote computer on the other side of the world, as it is to access a file on your computer, using a single interface like Windows Explorer. ActiveX will allow users of Microsoft Office to read and write Web pages using Office applications like Word, Excel and PowerPoint. Thus, while in the past someone was required to know HTML commands before they could design a Web page, the same environment used to produce everyday documents like business letters can now be used.

Browsing the Web

Navigating your way through the thousands of Web pages available was always meant to be simple; and for the most part, once you get going, it is: just as when you were a baby you could point at a toy and have someone bring it to you, all you need to do on the Web is point at something you want and click, and it arrives – only quicker and usually more successfully. The main stumbling blocks, however, lie in getting to know the environment provided by your Web browser software, and once that is done, in knowing where to start looking for the information that might interest you.

There is actually very little difference between the appearance of Netscape Navigator and Internet Explorer; the same goes for the way they function. It really could be no other way. If the World-Wide Web is a network of roads that you can explore, then your browser is the car you need to explore it – and just as any car has a windscreen, a dashboard, a steering wheel, an engine, four wheels, etc., any Web browser has a main window, a location box, a mouse interface and lots of technical stuff going on in the background. There would be just as little point in radically redesigning the Web browser as in trying to market a car that didn't have any of the components you would expect of one.

Consider the following screenshot, which shows a typical view from Internet Explorer:

The main window is where most of your attention will be focused. What you see here are the text and images laid out in just the way that the designers of the page you are looking at wanted (see the topic *HTML and Web page design* later). The white box you see above this window is the *location box*: the text you see here is the address, or URL (covered next). This contains all the information your browser needs to access the page you are looking at, and is the WWW equivalent of a postal address or telephone number. Several significant words in the text are underlined: these are the hot-links. If you rest your mouse pointer over any of these, you will see that the address in the status bar (the grey bar at the bottom of the screen) changes. The addresses you will see refer to the locations of the relevant linked sites. You could enter these by hand in the location box, if you wanted, but all you need to do – and this is the major reason for the spontaneity of the World-Wide Web – is click on the link with your mouse pointer. Graphics on the screen may also serve as links; if they do, you will see the text in the location box change to the linked page's http:// address.

The view of the World-Wide Web so far offered here has been rather limited: it is not simply a very sophisticated, electronic magazine. There are media used by the Web that cannot begin to be described in terms of magazine pages. For instance, on a seemingly ordinary-looking Web page you may come across a link to a site containing a Virtual Reality environment. The term 'Virtual Reality' has been bandied about enormously in the last few years, and not without good reason. The concept concerns the creation of virtual, electronic worlds through which you may 'travel', using a computer screen, or something like one, for your eyes. Many ambitious plans have been made for virtual reality, such as allowing people on opposite sides of the world to interact in a virtual environment as if they were in the same room as each other, and offering medical students a way to practise operating on virtual 'patients' before trying out their skills on the real thing. The virtual environments currently available on the Internet do not live up wholly to the lofty dreams of some science-fiction writers, but you can at least get a taster of what the future might be like by accessing sites like http://www.itl.nist.gov/div894/ovrt/OVRTmovies.html.

You will also find links to files containing video or audio clips: simply click on them with your mouse to access them. Some are designed to be played while you are connected to the Internet – this will require the presence on your system of the appropriate *plug-in* or alternative application software. For example, many sound recordings available on the Web are stored in RealAudio format. These allow you to play sound files in 'real time', as they are downloaded. To play them, you will need a special RealAudio player (get this, whether you are using Explorer or Navigator, from the site at http://www.realaudio.com).

URLs explained

Once you are connected to the Internet and have your Web browser running, you need somewhere to go with it; you need to access a Web site. In order to do this, you need an address, just as you would need the address of a shop or museum before you could visit it. The address of any Web site is known as a URL, or *Uniform Resource Locator*. While postal addresses begin with the specifics and end with the more general, URLs work in a convoluted fashion. Consider the following:

http://www.computerstep.com/1874029628.html

| 1 | 2 | 3 | 4 | 5 |

Part 1, http://, stands for "hypertext transfer protocol", and defines the type of service that is available at this address. You may often see URLs given without this, since it is more a command to your Internet application software to look for a certain type of information than an indication of where your browser is supposed to look. As a rule, whether or not you see http:// at the beginning of something that you know is a Web address, you should enter it in the *Location* box of your application software before the actual URL.

Parts 2-4 comprise the *domain name*, whose conventions are also used by other non-Web sites on the Internet. Part 2, www, stands, as you might expect, for World-Wide Web, and tells the browser that this is a Web site.

Part 3, computerstep, is the name of the site, equivalent to the house number or name in a postal address. This is Computer Step's Web site.

Part 4, com, denotes what sort of organisation this establishment is. In this case, we are told that it is *com*mercial. The number of different types of organisation is small, though the code used depends on whether the site is applicable internationally, or only to specific countries. The following table shows some you are likely to see most often:

Type of Organisation	UK Code	US/International Code
Academic	ac.uk	edu
Commercial	co.uk	com
Government	gov.uk (or govt.uk)	gov
Internet	net.uk	net
Non-profit	org.uk	org
Schools	sch.uk	sch

Most US sites, and many international sites, will have a single 3-letter code at position 4, as listed in the third column above. However, Web sites outside of the US often specify which country they are located in, with an additional element (separated, again, by a full stop) such as *uk*, *fr* (for France), or *au* (Australia).

At part 5, the URL address begins to get specific again. In this example, part 5 represents the name of the HTML file containing information on this book. However, many domains are divided into subdirectories, just as your hard drive is. A URL you see might include directions through several nested subdirectories, and at the end of this there may or may not be a file name. If there isn't one, then the Web server will automatically send your browser the default starting page for that location (often called *index.html*).

HTML and Web page design

After you've seen what can be achieved with the Web, you might dream of adding to it yourself. Most Web pages you see will look very professionally designed, using a mixture of text, pictures, perhaps illustrations, etc., and links to other pages. This might lead you to think that Web pages can only be created by people experienced in computer programming and design, but this is not so: like everything else related to the Web, page design was meant to be easy.

All Web pages are put together using a very simple language known as HTML *(HyperText Markup Language)*.

This is comprised of a small number of fairly intuitive codes that are inserted into the text you write in order to instruct Web browsers to apply certain effects to the text (such as underlining), or to place a picture or hot-link at a certain place on the page. You don't need any special programming tools to write HTML: you can create a Web page using a simple text editor like WordPad, or using a specially designed template in a word-processor such as Microsoft Word – though a more intuitive, visual approach is offered by dedicated HTML programs such as HoTMetaL (find it at http://www.sq.com) and Live Markup (http://www.mediatec.com/mediatech/download.html).

You can very easily instruct your Web browser to display HTML codes. If you have Netscape Navigator, with a Web page loaded, simply select *Document Source* from the *View* menu. In Internet Explorer, select *Source* from the *View* menu. You should see a screen containing no pictures or formatting, but merely long lines of text. Some pieces of text will be enclosed in <angled brackets>, and will initially make very little sense: these are the HTML codes. All the rest of the text will actually appear on the screen, though often with formatting changes applied.

HTML codes are very similar to the type of codes you had to enter on most old DOS word-processors, before the arrival of Windows, in order to get text to appear in italics, say, or bold. For example, the HTML code to turn italics on is <I>, while </I> turns italics off. So if you saw the following in a line of HTML code:

Italics <I>are</I> very effective <I>in moderation</I>.

...this would appear on a Web page as follows:

Italics *are* very effective *in moderation*.

All HTML codes work on this basis. A link to another page is established by inserting a special code followed by the Web address of the page; and a picture is inserted in a similar manner. You don't need specific permission from a Web site to provide a link to it from yours; if it's in the public domain, they'll be glad to have you show other interested people the way to their door.

This brief discussion of Web page design is no place for a listing of all the HTML codes you are likely to meet or need. Many Web sites provide an exhaustive list of such details, and also give tips as to how to make your Web pages as attractive and useful as possible. You might start at:

http://union.ncsa.uiuc.edu:80/HyperNews/get/www/html/lang.html

For a simple, friendly introduction to HTML programming, read the book *HTML in easy steps*, also published by Computer Step.

The main opening Web page is known as the Home page, and can include information about absolutely anything that interests its creator, or that the creator thinks might interest its readers. Many Home pages provide overview details of an organisation's products or business. Personal Home pages may display a person's hobbies, pictures of pets, and accounts of the family's latest holiday. Links are usually provided to other relevant sites. So someone with their own Web page might include a few paragraphs detailing recent developments in their attempts to breed newts, including pictures of any new arrivals, and then provide a hot-link to the Home page of the International Newt-breeders' Society.

To get some ideas about what to include on your Home page, browse around a few and maybe steal some ideas. One of the easiest ways of setting up a Home page is to save onto your hard drive the HTML code of a Web page you like, and then tailor it to your own needs, replacing bit-by-bit the text, pictures and links with relevant alternatives. If you do decide to do this, however, make sure that any Web page you intend to present as your own design is significantly different from that of anyone else:

you don't want someone, especially a large commercial organisation, accusing you of plagiarism.

Virtual servers

Once you've created your Web pages, you'll want to put them somewhere, so that others can have access. If yours is only a personal Home page, you'll probably take advantage of the small amount of free Web space that is likely to be offered by your service provider: the URL for your site would then be a subdirectory of the service provider's site. However, if the Web site you have created is for your business, you might not want others to know that your site is merely a sub-part of another company's site. One alternative to this is to set up your own server. This would require an expensive ISDN connection or leased line, and in addition to that, you would need lots of other expensive equipment. Naturally, this is not a viable alternative for most businesses, which would do well to consider using a *virtual server* instead.

If you have a virtual server, your Web pages are located in a subdirectory of a true server, owned by a company with a permanent Internet connection. However, this server is specially configured, using some clever Internet trickery, so that your subdirectory appears to be a server in its own right: instead of a URL like this...

http://www.serviceprovider.co.uk/users/mywebsite/

…you will have one like this:

http://www.mywebsite

Most large service providers offer this facility – at a price – and there are even companies whose sole purpose is to set up virtual servers.

When a virtual server, or a true server, is set up, it needs a domain name, and that domain name must be unique on the Internet. To ensure this, you must register it with the relevant authority. Domain names ending in *co.uk* should be registered with Nominet (http://www.nic.uk), while names ending in *.com* are the province of the American organisation Internic (http://www.internic.net). You don't have to use a *.co.uk* domain just because you are located in the UK: you're free to choose a *.com* domain for your virtual server if you want to give your site that international flavour.

E-mail

Despite the user-friendly wealth of knowledge and entertainment available on the World-Wide Web, the reason many people get connected to the Internet in the first place is so that they can send and receive e-mail (electronic mail). Perhaps this is because e-mail was around years before the Web was even a twinkle in the eyes of those Swiss nuclear physicists, and so its name has become more firmly established in popular culture; perhaps because it is simply an easier concept to understand, being analogous to postal mail. Among the main reasons for the enormous popularity of e-mail, though, are that it is extremely fast and cheap. While a letter sent by air and surface mail from the UK to America, say, might take a week to reach its destination, an e-mail will get there normally within a matter of minutes. Most service providers allow you to send as much e-mail as you want for free, so all you pay is the cost of your local telephone bill for the time it takes to connect to the provider and upload your previously-composed message or messages (a matter of seconds). So it costs just as little to send an e-mail to Australia as to someone half a mile down the road. E-mails rarely get "lost", and certainly never end up in a dead-letter office.

E-mail also compares favourably with voice telephone calls and faxes. The main problem with calling someone by telephone is that they have to be at their home, or office, or wherever it is you expect them to be, at exactly the time that you call them; and even if they are, then they may be on another line, talking to someone else. If you find yourself talking to an answering machine, the awkwardness of having to state your full reasons for calling, on cue and without feedback, normally means that the recipient will have to call you back later to clarify what exactly it is you wanted to say. The process of sending and receiving e-mail, however, is exactly the same for both parties whether the recipient is there or not. Fax machines are often busy, and when a fax does get through successfully, its quality is always considerably poorer than the original. An e-mail does not degenerate as it gets passed along the telephone lines, because it is composed entirely of digitally encoded characters. If one of the "packets" (the units of data into which all Internet transmissions are divided) of your e-mail failed to reach its destination because of some temporary glitch in the phone line, the software on the computer receiving the transmission would realise this, and request that the erroneous packet be sent again. All of this would happen automatically in a split-second, without you realising it had happened. Equally, an e-mail server never runs out of paper or toner, or gets switched off.

Thus e-mail takes the best features of the written letter, the telephone call and the fax, and, for most purposes, transcends them. E-mail is not simply a paperless letter, or a written telephone call; it encourages you to communicate your ideas in an excitingly different way. Telephone calls are generally thought of as extremely personal, but in practice they normally involve a catalogue of false starts and lines of thought that are not seen through to their conclusion; at least one of the parties usually puts down the telephone realising that some important thing wasn't said. E-mail, however, allows you to compose your thoughts logically and concisely, and to get everything said. If you put something clumsily first time, you can go back to it and correct it before the message is sent. Similarly, verbal conversations are subject to a whole range of tacit rules that must be adhered to if a speaker's utterances are not to be met with an embarrassing silence. As with written letters, e-mail allows one to be a little more adventurous; you can put across some subtle point that might work on more than one level. The recipient can then let this sink in before replying: things don't have to be taken so much at face value.

E-mail can improve on the written letter not just because it is transmitted faster. You are encouraged to keep your messages brief, partly because you are charged by the minute for using the telephone line to send an e-mail, and partly because you are faced with the prospect of being able to send your message as soon as you've typed the final paragraph – you don't have to wait until the next postal collection. Messages that might adopt a formal manner on paper – particularly business correspondence, with its imposing letterheads, and the idea that your letter should take up at least most of a side of A4 for it not to seem frivolous – are often realised with a much lighter tone when sent by e-mail: the medium is not loaded with expectations on the part of the sender.

On the other hand, there are some things that e-mail cannot do as well as a letter or telephone call, and these are realised mostly in the realm of personal, as opposed to business, communication. You can't hear the voice of your loved ones via e-mail; equally, you miss out on the expressiveness of someone's handwriting, and you can't doodle in the margin (though you can send encoded pictures). These, though, are minor gripes, and do nothing to hold back e-mail as the most effective means of communication for many purposes.

How, then, do you send an e-mail? The specifics vary according to what e-mail software you are using and who your service provider is, but there is still a simple, general pattern that you will follow, as outlined below. There are many e-mail programs available, such as Exchange, which comes with Windows, and Eudora (download an up-to-date version from the Web at http:// www.qualcomm.com). You can even send and receive e-mail using the mailing function of the web-browsers Netscape Navigator or Internet Explorer, though these lack some of the features of dedicated e-mail programs.

One important thing not always realised by people new to e-mail is that you don't have to be on-line, wasting your phone bill, while you write or read your e-mail. The idea is that you use your e-mail program to compose your message(s), then log on to your service provider. The e-mail program will then normally send your mail automatically, and check for any mail you have received. You then disconnect and use the e-mail program once again to read the mail you've been sent.

Just as when you are writing a letter you normally include your address and the address of the recipient, there are several items of information that need to be appended to an e-mail in order for it to be sent. Since you don't need to put an e-mail in an envelope, all of this information is attached to the top of the message itself, as a header. Your e-mail program usually represents this header as a number of boxes with blanks for you to fill in, which normally include the following:

To:	Cc:
From:	Bcc:
Subject:	Attachments:

You can enter the e-mail address of the recipient in the *To:* box manually, but most mail programs allow you to select an entry from an "address book", a menu of names and e-mail addresses that you have previously compiled. An e-mail address will look something like the following:

jsmith@provider.co.uk

The last two parts, .co.uk, should be familiar if you have read the topic on URLs – these tell us that the address is located at a commercial company in the UK. To the left of that, *provider* identifies the service provider (you might see *demon* or *aol* here, for instance), or the name of another company that has its own permanent Internet connection. Everything to the left of the @ sign distinguishes the holder of this e-mail address from all the other customers of this service provider. Most service providers allow their customers to choose this part of their address for themselves (a common format is an initial followed by a surname), but some assign arbitrary user identification codes to each of their customers. CompuServe, for instance, has given each user a 9-digit number in the past.

You don't normally have to enter anything in the *From:* box, since your name and e-mail address remain the same. Once you've entered this information in the program settings, the program automatically fills this in for you. Your full name normally appears before your address: this will appear on the message your recipient reads, but is not strictly a vital part of the address, and can be changed if you want, in the program settings.

In the *Subject:* line you can enter some clue as to what your message is about. If you subsequently receive a reply, the sender may choose to retain this subject heading, allowing you both to organise your messages effectively. This is especially useful if the correspondence evolves into a string of messages and replies. However, your e-mail will still get through if you leave the subject line blank.

Cc: stands for "Carbon copies". In this box you can enter the addresses of any other people you want to send mail to. Your service provider's mail system will then automatically send a copy of the message to those people – you don't have to worry about sending the same message the appropriate number of times. The information in the Cc: box will be seen by all the recipients.

If, on the other hand, you don't want people to know who their fellow recipients are, enter the addresses in the box labelled *Bcc:* (Blind carbon copies).

Attachments: is another optional category. This allows you to send binary files along with your e-mail message. These files can be anything, from computer programs, to picture files, to word-processor documents. Strictly speaking, e-mail can only contain ASCII text, and so in order for you to be able to send a binary file it must be encoded (i.e., all its '1's and '0's must be converted into letters, numbers and symbols using a system that will allow them to be converted back into binary form by your recipient). Your e-mail program will normally handle the process of encoding itself; all you have to do is specify which files to encode. However, there are several different methods of encoding, e.g., Uuencode and MIME, and you might come upon a problem if you find that you encode a file in a format that is not covered by your recipient's e-mail program. It is therefore often best to check before sending an encoded file that you are both using a commonly recognisable format.

You can read any normal ASCII email you receive from anyone without worrying that it might harm your computer, but beware of binary files sent to you by strangers. These could include viruses (see *Security and social issues on the Net* later, and *Viruses* in the Software section) sent maliciously by people who intend to do irreparable damage to your computer system.

Mailing lists

When you use e-mail, you are not limited to exchanging messages with a handful of friends and colleagues. Mailing lists allow you to correspond by e-mail with a group of perhaps hundreds or thousands of people who share the same interests as you, such as goldfish or golf. They work like this: you compose an e-mail message relating to the topic covered by a mailing list, then send your e-mail, not to a particular person or group of people, but to the list's e-mail address. This message is then received, usually not by a person, but by a computer program, which forwards your message to the e-mail addresses of everyone who has previously subscribed to the mailing list. Everyone then reads their mail, and if they have anything to contribute to a line of discussion, they send an e-mail in response. This results in a sort of free-for-all e-mail conference, in which everyone discusses broadly the same topic, divided into many subtopics, which may be discussed concurrently by different groups of people.

The computer program that manages most automated mailing lists is known as Listserv. You can tell if you're dealing with one of these by the fact that the name to the left of the @ in its e-mail subscription address will always be *listserv*. One very important thing to note here is that all Listserv mailing lists have two addresses: one to which you send all the messages that you would like the other list members to see (the mailing address), and one to which you send Listserv commands, like those needed to subscribe to or unsubscribe from a list (the subscription address). If you send an e-mail to the wrong address, you will either cause an efficient but inarticulate computer program to become very confused, or you will annoy perhaps hundreds of list members with an e-mail that contains meaningless computer commands.

Before you can subscribe to a mailing list, you need to know its name and its subscription address. You may often see such information given in computer magazines, but it is likely that you won't see the address of a list that covers exactly the topic that interests you. To remedy this, you can send an e-mail message to the following address, querying whether your subject of interest is covered by any Listserv processor world-wide:

listserv@earn-relay.ac.uk

To search for all the Listserv mailing lists on the subject of cats, for instance, you would send an e-mail to the above address, leaving the subject box blank, and containing the following single line:

list global/cats

You would then shortly receive an e-mail from the Listserv, listing all of the mailing lists on that topic. To receive a list of every Listserv mailing list (there are thousands), simply omit the "/cats" part.

To subscribe to a list that you have identified (there is no charge for this), you need to send an e-mail to the appropriate Listserv at the subscription address, asking that your name be added to the list. If your name is John Smith and you want to subscribe to the Acorn Computers Discussion List, whose mailing address is acorn-l@trearn, you would replace the part before the @ with "listserv", and thus send the following message to listserv@trearn:

sub acorn-l John Smith

Again, leave the subject line blank. The Listserv would shortly send you a message welcoming you to the list, and explaining how to go about contributing to the list's discussion. Subsequently, a copy of all mail sent to the list's mailing address would be sent also to you.

Usenet newsgroups

The term "newsgroups" is something of a misnomer, since the vast majority of them deal with chat or topical discussion, not news. In fact, Usenet newsgroups perform the same function as mailing lists, in that they are organised according to various interest groups, and allow people to send messages to those groups, which will then be seen by everyone else who chooses to read them. The only differences are that Usenet messages are distributed not by e-mail, but by a *Usenet feed*, which nevertheless uses the same medium as the Internet; that Usenet groups are not moderated, while some mailing lists are; and that you don't have to subscribe to a Usenet group to read its messages. If it takes your fancy one day to catch up on the latest in the world of bonsai, you can read the messages sent to rec.arts.bonsai, forget the newsgroup for a week or so, and then return to it without finding your mailbox clogged up with a backlog of messages – which is what would happen if you ignored your mailing list messages for a while without telling the Listserv to put them on hold. While a mailing list's messages are actually sent to its readers, newsgroup messages are simply put on display, allowing anyone with appropriate Usenet access to read them.

One particular advantage of Usenet is that its newsgroups are organised by subject type, not by the location at which they are managed – so it is much easier to find the groups that interest you. There are many Usenet categories, though most of them fall into one of the six following categories:

comp	Computing
sci	Science
rec	Recreation
soc	Social
misc	Miscellaneous
alt	Alternative

This is all fairly self-explanatory, except perhaps the need for both *misc* and *alt* as major categories. The reason for this is mostly historical. The first five categories in the list were established when Usenet was born, *misc* being used as a place for any subject that didn't fit under the other four. That was several years ago, and the structure of even the *misc* groups has become somewhat formalised and cast in stone. Usually nowadays, when a need for a new group comes along, it is concerned with some very arcane or scatological field of interest, and is immediately classified under the *alt* heading.

Other categories you will see include *news*, *talk* and *biz*. Newsgroup names are not restricted to one of these categories and a subheading. Indeed, many are denoted by several hierarchical levels, as with rec.arts.startrek.fandom.

Here is a list of some newsgroups that you might like to try out:

comp.ai	Artificial Intelligence
comp.dcom.modems	Modems
comp.virus	Up-to-date information on new viruses to look out for
sci.astro	Astronomy
rec.music.info	Information about where to find music, and discussion of it, on the Internet
rec.arts.cinema	Films and film culture
rec.pets	Discussion of pets
rec.travel.misc	Where to go, how to get there, and what to do when you're there
soc.culture.french	French culture
alt.alien.visitors	Speculation about visitors from other planets
alt.books.reviews	Literary reviews
alt.music.alternative	News on independent music
uk.misc	General discussion of British matters

In order to read the messages posted to a newsgroup, and to send your own messages, you need a service provider that provides a Usenet feed (i.e., one that allows you to connect to a selection of newsgroups) and a Usenet newsreader program. Free Agent is a popular one, and can be downloaded from http://www.forteinc.com/forte/.

While messages to a mailing list are organised into subtopics by means of the subject line in your e-mail header, Usenet topics are organised into *threads*. Your newsreader will provide you with a menu of all the threads covered by your newsgroup, stating how many messages have been sent under each one. These threads are not concrete, but are simply chosen by each message poster as a means of following on from someone else's argument; if no-one sends any messages under a particular thread, that thread will die off. To view the contents of a thread, click on it with your mouse, and use the functions particular to your newsreader to move through the thread, and between messages. If you should want to reply to a certain message, again select it, and click on the newsreader button or menu command provided for this purpose.

The concept of Usenet may seem like heaven to anyone with an interest which they want to discuss with people around the world. However, anyone who has spent some time using newsgroups will be aware of one particularly annoying aspect of Usenet: *spamming*. This is the posting of the same message indiscriminately to a large number of newsgroups (the term is also often applied to the practice of sending the same message to many e-mail addresses). The culprits of this are usually businesses attempting to use the Internet as a very efficient marketing medium: spamming is the Internet equivalent of sending mailshots, but is much cheaper. While every single postal mailshot sent by a company to prospective customers costs at least the price of a second-class stamp (in addition to the cost of stationery), it costs nothing to spam a hundred newsgroups, except the cost of the Internet connection while a single message is uploaded. Each of these newsgroups might be read by thousands of people.

Despite the apparently huge marketing potential of spamming, it is not as common as you might think. The reason for this is that most people do not like to be spammed; they don't want to waste their time reading or downloading advertisements for products or services that they have no interest in. Consequently, senders of spam messages are likely to receive a large number of protesting e-mail messages from their victims. In one case, the service provider of a spamming culprit was temporarily shut down when its computers collapsed under the weight of several thousand irate e-mail messages. For more on the subject of unacceptable Internet behaviour, see the topic on *Netiquette*, later.

FTP

If you want to download files – such as programs, pictures and text files – from the Internet, the chances are you'll use FTP *(File Transfer Protocol)* to do it. Files can be downloaded from Web sites in a much easier fashion, but a much wider range of software can be found at the longer-established FTP sites. An FTP archive is a sort of library of files, normally held at an academic or commercial site. The files are organised into a tree-like structure, like the files on your hard drive, and must be accessed by telling an FTP server (a kind of electronic librarian) where to go to look for the file. These files are normally freeware or shareware, meaning that you can use them either for free, or for a small charge if you decide that you like them.

Before the advent of the World-Wide Web, the only practical way to access FTP archives was to address the site directly using a dedicated FTP program. Now, many WWW pages contain links to FTP archives or specific files, enabling you simply to click on an icon to be transferred to the site and use your browser to download it. However, the FTP facilities provided by Web browsers are usually slower and more memory-greedy than dedicated FTP programs, so for the time being at least it's probably worth your while to use a program like WS FTP, which can be downloaded from the Web, at http://www.csra.net/junodj/.

To connect to an FTP site, you need to tell your software the address of its site. For example, you may see the following FTP address given in a magazine:

ftp://ftp.trumpet.com.au/winsock/twsk21f.zip

The first part, *ftp://*, simply indicates that this is an FTP file. If you are using dedicated FTP software, it is not necessary to specify this, though a Web browser such as Netscape Navigator will require this prefix, since it needs to know that it is not being told to access a Web page. The following part, *ftp.trumpet.com.au*, is the site name. Most FTP sites begin their address with *ftp*. The following part, *trumpet*, is in this case the name of the institution whose site you are accessing, and *com.au* shows that this is a commercial organisation located in Australia. You should enter all of the site name in the appropriate box (perhaps labelled "Host Name:") of your FTP client program.

The next pieces of information you have to enter are the user ID and password. The original purpose of FTP was to allow people to access and deposit files at remote sites where they had been registered as a user. Academics might use this system, for example, to exchange files with colleagues privately. Thus, if you were not registered at a site, you could not access the files there. The main use of FTP nowadays, however, is for public access. This means that anyone can access files from a site, without entering an account name or password. Despite this, the old conventions linger on, and an FTP server will request a User ID. In order to access the files available to the general public, you must enter "anonymous" in this box, and then use your e-mail address as your password. Once you have entered this information, you can tell your FTP client to connect to the server.

Since FTP archives are organised into a tree-like directory structure, it is not surprising that FTP programs operate in a very similar fashion to the general file management programs you already have on your computer, like Windows Explorer, or the older File Manager. To find a file in an FTP archive, you simply navigate through the directory structure by clicking on the directory names, select the file you want, then tell your FTP program to retrieve it. In the example given above, the file is not deeply embedded within a complicated directory structure: *winsock* is the name of a directory located at the first level of the archive, and *twsk21f.zip* is the name of a file located in that directory. This is an FTP version of Trumpet Winsock, whose alternative Web address was given earlier, under *Internet software*.

Netiquette

As with any social institution, there are rules regarding what is and is not acceptable behaviour on the Internet. If you're simply browsing a Web page, or downloading files via FTP, these rules don't really come into play. However, a good deal of the traffic on the Internet involves interpersonal communication, as with e-mail and Usenet newsgroups, and it is here that you should be aware of the complex matter of *netiquette*. Communication on the Internet differs from normal social interaction, in that the medium is largely textual, and so the nuances of voice and facial expression that might help to clarify someone's precise meaning and intentions in a face-to-face situation, or a telephone conversation, are lost. Another problem arises from the fact that Internet communication is spontaneous, though its effects are potentially permanent. For example, a rash, rude remark made in a vocal conversation can quickly be glossed over and forgotten by both parties; while an insult sent in the heat of anger to a Usenet newsgroup, almost as spontaneously, can be filed on someone's hard drive and kept indefinitely.

In order to prevent such electronic *faux pas*, you should keep in mind that, in a medium devoid of smirks, tongues-in-cheek, and comical tones of voice, any jocular or sarcastic remark you make on the Internet might be taken in a completely unintended way, as offensive, aggressive or just plain stupid. In an attempt to remedy this kind of problem, the society of the nascent Internet, composed largely of computer programmers, developed a system of abbreviations and *emoticons*, which were intended to express their true emotions.

If you study any newsgroup, mailing list or Internet Relay Chat discussion for a short while, you are likely to find the conversation peppered with seemingly meaningless sequences of letters, like "ROFL", "IMHO" and "FWIW". These in fact stand respectively for "rolling on the floor laughing", "in my humble opinion" and "for what it's worth". They are probably used as much to make initiates feel smugly superior, and to exclude bewildered new users ("newbies"), as to save typing time, and they clearly can't convey any emotion as subtly for instance as a well-judged smile. However, they are used quite often in certain areas of the Internet, so if you encounter them it would be worth your while to understand at least the most popular ones, if only to show to other, more seasoned users that you're not completely green. Some other abbreviations you might see are:

BBL	Be back later
BTW	By the way
FYI	For your information
GAL	Get a life
HTH	Hope this helps
IOW	In other words
IYSWIM	If you see what I mean
LOL	Laughing out loud
OIC	Oh I see
OTOH	On the other hand
PMFBI	Pardon me for butting in

The other type of emotional short-hand, emoticons, are often also known as *smileys*. This is because the first emoticon was a textual representation of a smiling face, as follows: :-)   (twist the book clockwise by 90° if you can't make it out). This is normally used to show that the writer is not entirely serious about what he or she has just said, and that perhaps the reader should search for an element of irony in the message before responding angrily. As such, emoticons can be a very useful tool, but some people tend to go a little overboard with them. Here are some others you might want to try, of varying advisability:

:-(	Sad face
;-)	Wink
:-D	Laughing
:-o	Shock
:-p	Tongue stuck out
:-&	Tongue-tied
}:>	Devil
0:-)	Angel

Despite these safeguards against Internet misunderstandings, things can go dreadfully awry, especially if someone is being wilfully malicious or arrogantly inconsiderate. An example of this is *trolling*, often seen in newsgroups. A troll is a deliberate attempt by someone posting a message to provoke a flood of indignant replies by people incensed that someone could be so controversial or rude. In fishing terms, *to troll* is to cast out a baited line from a boat and draw it back through the water in the hope of attracting fish as it passes. This special brand of Internet trolling might then sound a little masochistic, but the intention of the troller is probably to give himself a feeling of omnipotence and superiority in the knowledge that tens, perhaps hundreds, of people are wasting their time trying to browbeat someone into moral submission over a point that he probably doesn't care a thing about.

This flood of angry replies provoked by the troller, or by someone unwittingly making an inappropriate remark, is known as *flaming*. A *flame* is not a level-headed statement of one's difference of opinion, but a personal attack on someone, often sent angrily and spontaneously. Again, this may be the result of some misunderstanding of intention, owing to the lack of extraverbal cues available on the Internet. More often than not, though, people may simply be spoiling for an argument. A *flame war* is the phenomenon that occurs when someone who has been flamed does not admit defeat, but flames back. This may lead to counter-flames, and fresh flames from like-minded individuals who have been drawn into the argument. The various flaming parties may polarise, leading to a protracted flame war of several weeks, or even months, between two diametrically opposed groups. By this time the war has usually degenerated into gratuitous name-calling. Perhaps in years to come the development of new, effective emoticons might put an end to misunderstandings on the Internet, and hence eradicate this pointless fighting ;-).

Intranet

One of the newest and most exciting developments in the field of computer communications is the notion of "Intranet". While the Internet was born out of a desire to provide links *between* existing networks (e.g., between academic and military computer systems), Intranet focuses on communication *within* networks. This begs the question, why do we need to think about such small-scale matters when it is already possible, and very easy, to communicate with computers anywhere in the world? The main reason for the amount of attention given by many organisations in the world of computing (particularly Microsoft) to the concept of Intranet is the growing number of businesses that are coming on-line. While aspects of the Internet, such as the World-Wide Web, are ideally suited to the individual seeking information, software or communication with other individuals, little provision is made for organisations (such as multinational businesses) with a number of branches nationally and world-wide, whose members wish to communicate efficiently with each other. Clearly, any office with a computer, a modem and a telephone line can send an e-mail to any other similarly equipped office, but if a company's London branch, say, wants to send a memo to all of that company's other branches world-wide, or to hold a conference with members of those other branches, then using the Intranet is the best way of doing this.

Any office with a number of computers is likely to use a LAN, or *Local Area Network* (normally a network of cables running between each computer in the office) to link those computers together, in order that they may exchange data (such as word-processor files) with each other spontaneously, without requiring the transfer of that data to floppy disk. Such an office is increasingly likely to be connected to the Internet, allowing it to communicate in an appropriate fashion with customers, suppliers and associated branches. However, in the past, the interfaces used to interact with local computers via the LAN on the one hand, and remote computers via the Internet on the other, were completely separate – although the data being exchanged might be exactly the same. The idea of the Intranet is that copying a file from a computer perhaps on the other side of the world should be just as easy as exchanging data across a local network, or from one directory to another on the same computer, and that all of these processes should use the same interface, thus integrating both systems seamlessly. The interface used for Intranet communication will be something like the Windows Explorer.

Microsoft are supporting the development of Intranet communication by producing software that includes World-Wide Web technology. For instance, Office 97, Microsoft's very popular suite of programs including word-processor, spreadsheet and presentation applications, enables the user to produce a document such as a brochure, and easily publish it on the Internet, or a company Intranet, at the click of a button. New versions of Windows will incorporate the Web browser, Internet Explorer, with the operating system, using a new Windows Active Desktop. Thus, communication and day-to-day Windows activities such as file management will be a part of the same process, reflecting the nature of today's globally-networked business environment.

Security and social issues on the Net

One feature of the Internet that many people find attractive is its remarkable level of public accessibility, and lack of control by any central Internet administrator (after all, the whole point of the Internet is that it *has* no centre) leading to an unprecedented degree of freedom in social and educational interaction. For example, while a totalitarian government might impose restrictions on the information available to its citizens via media such as newspapers, television and libraries, anyone in such a country with access to the Internet is privy to a wealth of knowledge tainted only by the personal biases of the individuals who submit it.

However, the openness of the Internet has a corollary that has received an enormous, and disproportionate, amount of media attention in recent years: the same freedom that allows the innocent individual to roam the electronic highways and byways of the world in search of whatever information he or she chooses, also allows the not-so-innocent cracker, or infiltrator of supposedly secure computer systems, to access information about organisations or members of the public that should be confidential.

An issue that concerns most users of the Internet is the privacy of e-mail. An electronic message sent to someone via the Internet might pass between any number of computers in different parts of the world in order to reach its destination. This makes it relatively easy for someone knowledgeable enough in the field of computer communications to intercept the mail at any of these nodes and read it. Most e-mail messages probably contain only the sort of information that anyone would be prepared to shout in the street, or send on a postcard (e.g., greetings, social chit-chat, technical discussions), but at any rate, most people would be a little miffed to learn that some nosy or malicious person had been eavesdropping on them. However, it is very unlikely that you would ever learn that someone had been reading your e-mail, since the tell-tale signs that would suggest that someone had been reading a letter sent by the postal system (e.g., torn and resealed envelopes, or simply mail that was expected but didn't arrive) are clearly not available electronically.

More importantly, perhaps, there is the question of credit-card fraud as a result of someone reading e-mail in which you had disclosed your credit-card number in order to purchase something, or gaining access to similar information that you might have submitted to an electronic shopping service's Web-site. There is still no established, perfectly fail-safe means of protecting yourself against this sort of fraud, though a number of developments come pretty close. Netscape Navigator, for instance, offers its users the ability to perform "secure transactions" with a few clicks of the mouse button; the processes of encryption and decryption are handled automatically.

However, if you want to send confidential e-mail on the Internet, the current standard is to encrypt it using a program called PGP *(Pretty Good Privacy)*. This is based on the same theory of encryption used by Web browsers like Navigator, employing a system of *public keys* and *private keys.* These keys are coded sequences of data used to encrypt and decrypt your messages. It works as follows: when you install PGP on your system, the setup program asks you to enter a pass phrase. This should be easily memorable – since you should not keep a written record of it – though it should not be possible for anyone else to deduce what it is. This is then used to generate your private key, which subsequently can only be unlocked by entering your pass phrase.

Once the setup process is complete, you end up with a public key and a private key. You then distribute the public key to anyone who might want to send you secure mail, but keep the private key only on your computer. Then, when someone sends you mail, they use your public key to encrypt the message, generating a file that looks like a sequence of random ASCII characters: they send this to you as they would any normal e-mail. This file, however, cannot be decrypted using your public password; a complicated method of encryption renders it unreadable without your matching private key, which no-one else has access to, and your pass phrase. You can also "seal" your message with your key, allowing the recipient to see whether or not the message has been intercepted and tampered with en route. Clearly, the public key and private key are related – though by extremely complicated mathematical procedures, and with the added complication of your password – and it is theoretically possible for someone with a very powerful computer and plenty of time on their hands to decipher even a PGP-encrypted message. However, unless you are in the habit of sending e-mail containing information that is a threat to national security, it is unlikely that anyone would want to spend their time deciphering your mail.

If you want a list of sites from which you can obtain PGP, send an e-mail to the following address, leaving the subject line and message space blank:

pgpinfo@mantis.co.uk

If you're resident in the UK, or indeed anywhere outside the USA, you should not obtain your copy of PGP from any USA site. PGP has been classed by the US Government as a munition (i.e., ranking alongside military weapons and ammunition) because of its supposed threat to national security, since the use of such encryption makes it hard for the Government to keep tabs on its citizens. It is illegal to export munitions without permission of the Government, and so the developer of PGP, Phil Zimmerman, is effectively breaking the law every time someone from outside of the USA downloads a copy of the program. The list you'll get from the e-mail address given above names several non-USA sites from which you can download PGP without anyone breaking the law – but the version you'll get is likely to be a cut-down version of what is available in the States, in order to circumvent this bizarre piece of legislation.

Unfortunately, this interception of electronic messages is not the only way in which personal or corporate security can be compromised on the Internet. It is also possible for the criminals to come to you, by infiltrating your system, either directly if you have a server permanently connected to the Net, or indirectly by allowing you unwittingly to accept such gremlins as viruses and Trojan horses.

The ordinary member of the public, who temporarily connects to the Internet once in a while via a service provider, should have no fear of someone hacking into their computer while they are on-line to read all the personal documents on their hard drive and mess about with their system files: the software you use to interface with the Net, be it a Web browser or an FTP client, should not allow anyone to access your computer, except to send files or any other electronic information that you specifically request.

However, if your company has a permanent connection to the Internet, with a leased line and a computer running a server program 24 hours a day, then clearly the intention is to provide limited access to external users – perhaps so that customers can learn more about what your company sells. The question is, how much access can those users actually gain, given a certain degree of technical know-how, and the time it takes to learn the workings of your server? People who gain unauthorised access to computer systems are known as *hackers* or *crackers*. In the early days of computer communications, when access to computer networks was limited mostly to the military and scientific community, and when indeed the purpose of those networks was to exchange information that might have been best kept out of the hands of the general public, it was possible for some exceptionally motivated individuals to access what should have been top-secret information. However, those organisations with information worth guarding (like the military) are nowadays considerably more aware of the threat to their systems posed by crackers, and are unlikely to keep any particularly sensitive information on any computer that can be accessed via the Internet. The attentions of crackers, then, are directed more towards the growing number of commercial organisations coming on-line, whose restricted information, such as lists of credit-card numbers, might offer the possibility of financial reward to anyone gaining access to it.

The usual way of paying for something on the World-Wide Web is to enter information into a 'form'. This is a kind of dialogue box, very similar to the sort of thing into which you enter your settings for any Web browser or e-mail program – except a form at a commercial Web site would ask for information like your name, credit card number, and the details of the products you want to purchase. This information is then held – for a short period at least – on a database used by the site's server. No-one involved in these kinds of transaction, be they customer or supplier, is ignorant of the threat posed by crackers to the security of such databases, and consequently they are very well protected – but there have in the past been scares concerning just such violations of security, which should not have been possible.

The most widely used method of protecting confidential information on the Web from unauthorised access is to create a *firewall*. The seemingly paradoxical idea behind this is that the computers holding such information are isolated from the Internet, while still being capable of receiving customer information from it. The server computer, which does all the communication with outside users, acts as the 'middle-man', receiving any confidential information, but not storing it: it passes this information on, via an internal link, to the organisation's main computers, which otherwise have no connection to the Internet, and which are not programmed to respond to any computer other than the server. The question remains whether an infiltrator's computer might, for instance, be able to 'impersonate' the server, in order to access the internal computers, but measures against such attacks are constantly being developed by benevolent Internet organisations such as FIRST *(the Forum of Incident Response and Security Teams)* and CERT *(the Computer Emergency Response Team)*. Details about these can be found from FIRST's Web site, at http://www.first.org/.

While the question of the security of confidential information you might provide over the Internet is certainly a matter of concern, you should not lose too much sleep over it, since the organisations to which you supply the information doubtless spend a good deal of time and effort trying to provide a secure service; it is, after all, in their interest to do so, if they value their customers. There is, however, another area of Internet security in which you should be particularly vigilant – the threat of viruses – because here you are more or less on your own. Viruses are also covered in the *Software* section, but some mention of them is warranted here, as certain types of virus are particular to the Internet environment.

A virus is a type of program whose function is to cause some disruption in the functioning of a computer. This may take the form of an irritating message that, unbidden, displays itself across your computer screen on a certain date, or, more seriously, might attempt to wipe or corrupt some or all of the files on your system. Just like a real-world virus, a computer virus has the ability to spread itself to other organisms – other computers. In the past, before long-distance computer communication was common, viruses spread themselves via local networks and floppy disks. The arrival of the Internet, however, has provided them with a much more dynamic means of transmission.

A virus does not happen on its own – it is not the result of some anomalous electronic mistake that passes itself on to other computers by suggestion; nor is it a new form of electronic life that is only doing the same as the rest of us – trying to survive – and might deserve protection as an endangered species. No: computer viruses are created by malicious programmers who simply want to inject a little irritation or havoc into the lives of computer users they have never met. It is quite easy to see why some individuals might want to break the law in order to gain knowledge of your credit card details: they want your money. The reasons for a programmer to develop a virus, however, are somewhat harder to discern. On several occasions in the past, large, wealthy organisations, such as banks, have been targeted, and have had their computers infected with viruses designed to change or destroy financial information on a preset date unless a large amount of 'ransom' money is submitted in return for a password which will render the virus harmless. Such organisations now apply much tighter security to their computer systems. However, the independent computer user should have nothing to fear from such big-business viruses, which are designed exclusively to affect computers running software that no-one outside the targeted organisation would have any cause to use. The viruses from which lone Internet users should protect themselves are probably best likened to a programmer's version of graffiti, or a type of calculated, orchestrated vandalism – designed to profit the perpetrator's ego rather than his bank account.

One much-publicised type of Internet virus is the *Worm*. This doesn't cause any actual damage to a computer, except by virtue of the fact that it is there, lurking on the system, and taking up vital hard-drive space and memory. It will copy itself from one Internet-connected computer to another without permission, and can potentially be inhabiting thousands of computers around the world within a matter of minutes. From these computers it may copy itself back to computers that it has already reached, possibly duplicating itself indefinitely.

Another commonly used term in the field of viruses is *Trojan horse*. Just like the mythical wooden horse built by the Greeks to infiltrate the city of Troy, and offered as a present, it at first appears to be harmless, masquerading as a useful program that users should want to run on their computers. When they do execute the file, however, the virus, like the Greek warriors, creeps out and does its damage.

A *time-bomb* is designed to be left on a computer, lurking invisibly, often until a certain date, say April 1, arrives. When it does, the virus suddenly and unexpectedly 'explodes', often in tandem with all the other computers that have been infected, possibly corrupting important files, and displaying a message informing the user of what has just happened.

Electronic *bacteria*, like their organic counterparts, simply want to reproduce... and reproduce, taking up as much hard-disk space and memory as they can. Other than this, they do no damage, but it is possible for a computer with a completely full memory and hard drive to be put out of action. At the very least, bacteria are an annoying, and often inexplicable, drain on a computer's resources.

As with any type of virus, those that you might contract from your travels on the Internet are best dealt with by preventative measures. First of all, you should perform regular backups of all the important data on yourcomputer. Then, if some of your files are corrupted, you can replace them. If worst comes to worst, and your whole computer system is rendered useless by a virus, you can then always start from scratch: re-install your operating system and all your programs from the CDs/disks you bought them on, then copy back your important data.

Once you've made your backups, you may want to take measures towards preventing a virus from ever doing any damage to your computer, by purchasing some anti-virus software. Programs of this sort, such as *PC-cillin*, can either scan your whole system for the presence of a virus, or analyse selected files. You might then individually analyse every file you download from the Internet before you use it, and then, just to be safe, check all the files on your hard drive every week – or instruct your software to monitor your system constantly for the presence of viruses. Beware, however: anti-virus programs can often only detect viruses that were around when the programs were developed; newly developed gremlins using different methods of infiltration might slip past unnoticed.

One final tip on avoiding viruses from the Internet: be discriminating about the sort of places from which you download files. A large Web site such as Microsoft's is likely to be very well screened by anti-virus software much more powerful and up-to-date than your own, and anyway most of the software you'll find there comes from its own programmers. On the other hand, files submitted to the *binaries* sections of Usenet newsgroups, to which any Internet user can add, should be treated with circumspection.

From what has been said in the preceding paragraphs, it should be apparent that, given suitable conditions and a lack of knowledge or vigilance on the part of the computer user, a virus can do a great deal of damage to a computer's files. Viruses are consequently the subject of much hysteria on the Internet, and this hysteria has been played upon by many people who are interested in having a joke at the expense of others. Take, for example, the story of the *Good Times* virus. This concerns a virus that is transmitted by e-mail, the offending messages having the alluring subject line 'Good Times'. Supposedly, anyone reading such a message automatically unleashes a virus on their computer that will cause untold havoc. In fact, such a virus has never existed, and it is not possible to contract a virus simply by reading e-mail – though it is now possible to attach executable binary files (typically with the extension *.exe*) to e-mail messages, and these should be treated with as much caution as any such file you might download from other sources, particularly if you don't know the sender. A virus can only be contained in an executable file; files that contain mere data that is to be read by another program, such as text or picture files, can do your computer no harm.

Having said this, it is possible that certain files other than those with an *.exe* extension might contain commands that could do damage to your files. Many programs, for example, allow the user to define and use *macros*, which are short sequences of commands within the application that otherwise might require many repetitive keystrokes or calculations. Microsoft Word allows users to define moderately sophisticated macros, which can access files on the system in order to load, save etc. It could be possible to write a macro that manipulates the files on a

computer system, possibly deleting vital files. This macro
could then be attached to a Word document, and sent via
email or uploaded to a public-access repository of files –
and then run by someone who thinks they are simply
taking advantage of someone else's labour-saving
ingenuity. Naturally, a dangerous macro of this sort
would not be picked out by an antivirus program, since
Word macros have every right to be on someone's PC.

The future

It is currently very fashionable in the media to attempt to
predict the direction that will be taken by the Internet in
the future. We are told that before the century is out, we
will be using the Internet to communicate with friends,
shop, work from home and entertain ourselves. Science
fiction writers envisage a situation where a network of
supercomputers sustains a virtual environment which
people connect to and treat as if it were just another part
of the real world. Harbingers of digital doom inform us
that we are in danger of becoming a world of media-
addicted vegetables, capable of making physical effort
only to turn on a computer where we will find a world in
which our desires are sated at will, without our expending
any energy, the only cost to us being the elements of
existence that make our lives worth living in the first place.

Virtual reality will doubtless grow in complexity and in the sophistication of the environments it is capable of producing. Already it is possible on the Internet to enter a virtual world, a simulated 3-dimensional environment you can view with your computer screen, where you adopt a computer 'body' known as an *avatar*. This is really just a computer image, usually bearing no resemblance at all to your physical body, which is used to represent your position in the virtual world. You manoeuvre your avatar around that world, identifying other visitors by their avatars, and interacting with them. At the moment, this interaction really amounts to the kind of chat that you would find on Internet Relay Chat, or CompuServe's CB Simulator. However, some virtual worlds allow visitors to modify their environment, creating 'buildings' they have designed, which can then be visited by others. It is possible to envisage the growth of communities in such a world, from small electronic hamlets to complex cities, where people, irrespective of their physical distance from each other, can socialise and go about their business without fear of being mugged in the street or getting caught in a traffic jam.

Clearly, a virtual world can be no substitute for the physical world we all know and love. We at least need to eat and drink, and most people would not find the prospect of sitting in front of a computer screen all day, or wearing some virtual reality headset, very attractive. However, if we view virtual environments simply as an effective means of communicating instantaneously with friends, relatives, colleagues, etc., without the need to spend perhaps hours travelling to meet them, the whole idea needn't be so scary. A 3-D virtual conference room, for instance, could be visited by business colleagues from a number of different countries, who could present reports to each other, show video presentations, and display performance charts without actually being in the same room as each other. This surely beats anything that could be achieved by telephone or fax.

It may be some time before virtual worlds exist with the necessary sophistication to enable such global communication for more than a handful of people: if the necessary communities are to exist as anything more than 3-D chat-lines, or multi-user flight-simulators, then they need to be visited and developed by many people who care about the environment they are creating – and there is still plenty of scope for the popularity of the Internet to increase. However, in the immediate future, and given only the current Internet technology and population, we can expect to see, for instance, a much more complete integration of e-mail into the business world. For reasons given earlier, under the topic of E-mail, this is the ideal method of communication for most business needs, and while it is already hugely popular in many professions, not enough people or businesses have Internet accounts for it to be possible to take it for granted that someone you might want to contact has an e-mail address, just as you would take it for granted that someone has a telephone.

One of the main criticisms thrown at the Internet currently is that it is insecure (see the topics on *E-mail* and *Security and social issues on the Net*), making it possible for confidential information to be intercepted by those with the appropriate technical know-how and lack of morals. While this threat probably does not deserve the amount of hysteria that has been devoted to it, it is certainly an issue that needs to be given attention if more people (perhaps those with less knowledge of computers, who might easily be swayed by reports of credit card numbers being stolen over the Internet) are to feel confident enough to use the Internet as the popular method of mass communication that it deserves to be.

Another focus of concern is the fact that certain unsavoury material, such as pornography, can be found on the Internet, and might easily be accessed by children. Since this is a medium with which children are likely to be more familiar than their parents, it is no surprise that many parents feel threatened by the presence in their homes of a source of such virtually limitless information. Many computer programs (mostly concerned with the World-Wide Web and newsgroups) are already available which purport to allow parents to censor the kind of information that their children can access. This relies on the creators of potentially unsuitable Web pages performing self-censorship on their work, grading their work according to a universally agreed scale (on grounds of content, explicitness, etc.) and coding this information in such a way that a program on a computer used by a child could filter out any of the categories deemed by the parents as unsuitable. One such program is Net Nanny. The effectiveness of these programs, however, is questionable, particularly since they rely on the cooperation of the creators of Internet resources in censoring their own work. The Internet is inherently anarchic and resistant to censorship or government by any central body, and so it is difficult to imagine quite how any real control of content could be brought into effect. It is relatively easy to censor the output of, say, a television station, since there are only a limited number of stations in an area, which must have schedules, and which are governed by watchdog organisations whose sole function it is to control what they produce. A Web page, however, can be set up by anyone with a computer and a telephone line, for free, meaning that it would be impossible for any national or international body to either censor the thousands upon thousands of Web pages that exist, or to force their creators to self-censor them.

One of the main problems that the world of global digital communications faces in expanding itself is the fact that many people have only a vague idea of what the technology involves, or even of what a modern computer is capable of doing. Frightened by this vague, faceless ogre of computer technology, which they somehow feel has more control over their lives than they would wish, they often choose simply to ignore it, and go back to watching the television. However, one aspect of digital communications that any telly addict can understand without giving it the least effort is *Video On Demand*. This is essentially a technology that would allow anyone to request any film or television programme to be shown, not according to some national or regional broadcast timetable, but exactly when the individual viewer wants to see it – just as you can visit a Web page whenever you want, or download an FTP file.

The main stumbling block for Video On Demand lies in the fact that any film, with its hours of colour images and high-quality sound, comprises an enormous amount of data. If you were to attempt to download a full-length digitised film, of the quality you would find on, say, a Video CD, to your computer with your modem, it would take hours. In fact, the concept of Video On Demand does not use the normal telephone line, but a special digital line (see the earlier discussion on *ISDN*), which has the wide bandwidth required to facilitate the transmission of such huge amounts of data. The viewer does not need a PC with a keyboard, but a dedicated VOD receiver, which would probably be operated by means of a menu system which would appear on the television screen. The main problem in getting such a scheme off the ground lies in the fact that, as with any new technology, the receiving equipment needed for it will initially cost an exorbitant amount, and that most homes in most countries are not currently supplied with a digital fibre-optic communications line.

Tests of prototype VOD systems have not proved very popular. Maybe this is related to the cost, or maybe people simply like the idea of being spoon-fed with their media. Whatever the case, it remains that the technology involved in Video On Demand, and that used by the

Internet, are very similar: both use digital communications, both offer some means of downloading data... The technologies of public broadcasting and personal computer communications are gradually converging. It is likely that some time in the perhaps not too distant future, the two will merge into a single medium, accessible using a single type of terminal, yet allowing people to choose the way they like their information. Those who like a steady, reliable diet of the same form of entertainment, like a soap opera that has daily episodes, should be able to receive that, as it is produced, or a month later; while those who prefer to seek out information or entertainment on a topic that they know will not be covered by public broadcasts should be able to access the dedicated sites that will best serve their needs.

Upgrading Your PC

nevitably, there will come a time when some aspect of your PC either breaks down or becomes outdated. Your computer has very few moving parts, but even solid-state microchips occasionally decide to stop working, and the connections on printed circuit boards may weaken. Computer technology continues to grow exponentially, and as it does, newer, better computers are being produced frighteningly quickly. No matter how much care you take in choosing a new computer, you can rest assured that within a matter of months you will be able to buy one with significantly better features for the same price or less.

The answer to this is not to throw away your broken or outmoded computer in a fit of rage, but to take it apart. PCs were designed to a modular scheme, allowing you to replace one bit of it without having to discard all the others, or to add a new module entirely. One option available to you in such a situation is to take your PC back to the dealer. However, for many purposes, you could do the job just as well as any professional, with a screwdriver, a few moments' contemplation, and a basic knowledge of what you can expect to find inside your PC's case. This section aims to be that guide. Even if you do decide that something is beyond you, and that you want to get it done at a computer repair shop, much of the information you find here will at least enable you to talk knowledgeably about what you want done, or to decide what to upgrade.

Deciding what to upgrade

You may already have an idea about which elements of your computer system are in greatest need of repair or upgrading. If your monitor suddenly gives a pop and starts smoking, you know which bit you have to replace. But the matter of diagnosing just which of the many interrelated components of a PC might be causing your problem is usually not so simple. For example, if you find some of your programs running too slowly, your suffering might be caused by a tired, old CPU, by a lack of memory, or by a hard drive with a long access time. How should you know which to change?

One answer is to use some diagnostic software. This will set itself up on your system and perform a battery of tests designed to monitor the performance of your PC with relation to processor speed, disk access time, etc., and will establish just how efficiently all the different components of your computer are working and talking to each other. Any conflicts between hardware and software, or between two different pieces of software, should be detected, and a suggestion made as to which of the available options is most likely to solve your problem. Not every aspect of the functionality of your PC is set purely by the specifications of your hardware: very many parameters pertaining to the basic running of your PC are set in system files. These may, for instance, determine the trade-off between the amount of upper memory available to programs, and the effective speed of the running of those programs. Diagnostic software should be able to determine whether or not the current system settings on your computer are the most suitable for your requirements; it will also check the performance of peripherals, such as your printer, modem and CD-ROM drive, and determine whether or not they conflict with each other or with the main system unit.

Despite this, the need for such independent diagnostic software has become less and less as Windows has established itself as the operating system running on most computers. Most new hardware you are likely to buy for a PC nowadays is likely to employ Plug'n'Play technology, which automates the process of installing new hardware, avoiding most device conflicts caused by poor allocation of resources (see the Plug'n'Play topic later). If, however, you do experience some problem, you have the option of running the Windows Hardware Conflict Troubleshooter – see the topic *Installing hardware via Windows* later in this section.

Upgrading hardware

The hardware of a PC can be broken down into several distinct parts, each with a more or less specific function. The essential parts are as follows:

- Memory – when you run an application such as a word-processor, the data necessary for the basic functioning of the program are transferred from the hard drive, where they are stored, to the memory. The CPU then accesses the information held temporarily in the memory in order to run the program. If you find that your computer slows down to a crawl when running several large, complicated programs at once, you probably need some extra memory.

- CPU *(Central Processor Unit)* – this is the 'brain' of your computer, the part that does most of the important number-crunching. Since so many other aspects of the PC's functioning rely on the CPU, it is the most complicated part to upgrade: e.g., try to replace a 486 CPU with a Pentium chip, and you could find yourself having to buy many other new peripheral parts.
- Hard drive – the medium used to store the bulk of the files that your computer needs to function, from basic system files, to application files, to the data used by those applications. The average capacity of hard drives has increased enormously within the last few years, and if you are still buying new, space-hungry software for an older machine, the chances are you're very short of drive space.
- Monitor/Video card – since the visual display is the major medium your computer will use to communicate with you, you should consider whether or not your current display is doing what you need it to. If you only use your computer for simple tasks such as accounting and word-processing, you can get away with an old, fairly primitive (by today's standards) VGA monitor. On the other hand, if you're into desktop publishing or graphic design, or if you want

to put together a multimedia system capable of running detailed video clips and high-resolution, multi-coloured graphics, then you'll want to invest in a large-size SVGA monitor with a sizeable amount of video RAM. While your monitor is housed in a separate box from the rest of your PC, the video card that drives it is located, along with the rest of the hardware, in the casing of the main system unit. For more details on this, see *Monitor* in *The PC Unravelled* section.

- Sound card – unless you have one of these, your PC will struggle to emit anything better than a feeble beep whenever it wants to communicate with you audibly. A sound card can be used to play high-quality music, speech or other sound effects, and also, via a microphone, to record sounds of your own that you might want to use in multimedia applications. Almost all programs produced nowadays will benefit from being used with a sound card. For further information, see *Sound card* in *The PC Unravelled* section and *Multimedia* in the *Software* section.

- CD-ROM drive – virtually any software produced nowadays is available on CD-ROM. If you install all your software from floppy disks, you will be used to a prolonged installation process, in which you are required to swap disks every two or three minutes. A CD-ROM, on the other hand, offers a much faster access time; all of the installation data can be held on one CD-ROM; and you will often be given a much wider range of supplementary data (e.g., clip art) than could sensibly be provided on floppy disks.

- Modem – buying one of these allows your computer to talk to others via the telephone line, opening up to you a whole new world of information, so much that in a lifetime you could never absorb what is currently available, let alone what is to be provided in the future. For much more on the Internet and the World-Wide Web, see Section 5.

Once you've decided what exactly needs to be upgraded on your PC, you have done most of the hard work; you will most likely find the process of installing or replacing the new components to be surprisingly easy. To open up the PC's case, you'll need a screwdriver, which you can usually then put aside until you're ready to close the case back up: most hardware upgrading is a matter simply of pushing the connectors of a card into a socket.

Before you reach for your screwdriver, though, there is one thing that you should consider when buying and installing hardware, which should help to make the process much easier...

Plug'n'Play

Plug'n'Play technology, first introduced with Windows 95, allows new device cards you install in your PC to determine their own settings, rather than have you tell them what settings to take. This makes it much easier for you to install and upgrade new hardware on your computer. You simply plug a new component (such as a modem or a graphics card) into an available expansion slot, and it is ready to work straight away – you don't have to go through some laborious setup process, describing to an installation program all the specifications of your existing computer hardware. This is because Windows manages all of the communication between your various hardware components, and in most cases allots the appropriate amount of system resources to the different components as they are required. When a new card is plugged in, it determines what settings are already used by existing cards, and will only set itself up to use settings that are free, or settings that can be freed by rearranging the configuration of the existing cards. Most new hardware for sale nowadays, from graphics cards to modems, will carry the Plug'n'Play symbol, in advertisements and on the packaging; you should be wary about buying hardware that does not claim to be Plug'n'Play.

Opening up the case

This is not the traumatic experience that you might expect it to be. As has already been said, PCs are designed to allow you to change and install new parts of them easily. This is especially true if yours is a tower case, as opposed to a desktop unit. A desktop is longer than it is tall, and the monitor normally sits on top of it, while a tower unit is a tall box offering much easier access to its insides, making it easier to get at the ports and expansion slots into which you slot new components.

The first thing you should do when installing new hardware is to make sure that your PC is turned off using the switch on the computer's casing. If the mains outlet into which you plug your computer has a switch, turn it off here, too, but don't remove the plug from the wall. This will shut off the electric current, but will mean that the computer is still earthed, and so more capable of discharging any static electricity that you introduce to it when you start fiddling with its insides. (If the mains outlet doesn't have a switch, you should unplug your computer completely.)

Now you should make plenty of space for yourself. Unplug the monitor, and put it out of the way; you should never need to open up its casing. Unplug all of the other cables from the back of the computer, except the power-supply cable (see above), then turn the system unit around so that you have a clear view of its back, and all of the sockets there. Now locate the screws that keep the cover in place. Whether you have a desktop or a tower unit, these should only be located around the very outside edge of the back of the computer; don't remove any screws on the panel holding all of the sockets, unless you want some of your computer's insides to fall out of place. There are usually around 7-12 screws. Keep these safe while you're working, and don't get them mixed up with any screws you might remove subsequently.

Now, take hold of your computer's external casing, and gently try to pull it backwards and upwards. It should slide away without too much effort. If it doesn't, check that there aren't any screws still fixing the case to the computer's chassis – don't force it.

What you see inside your computer's case may initially seem daunting, but you can quickly begin to separate components into several different sections. First, try to relate what you are used to seeing on the outside of your PC to what you now see inside. Locate your floppy disk drive's door, then follow it back to the metal box that is the drive itself. Somewhere near this, you should see another box of similar shape and size, only with no opening onto the face of your PC – this is your hard drive.

It should have a circuit board attached to it, which holds some of the hardware that controls its functioning.

On the back of your PC, near all the sockets, there should be a metal grille, through which you might be able to spy a fan. This is used to help cool down the power supply unit (PSU), which converts the alternating current it draws from the mains into the direct current your PC needs. The power supply unit is hard to miss: it's contained in a large metal box next to the fan.

Now, on the back of the computer, find the socket into which you plug your monitor's signal cable (not the power cable, which is probably plugged in near to the PSU). Behind this, inside the casing, you will find a card which extends backwards into the computer. This is your video, or graphics card. Similarly, if you have a sound card, you should be able to locate it by tracing backwards from where you plug in the cables from your speakers; if you have an internal modem, trace backwards from the telephone connector cable.

Apart from all these peripheral cards, you will see one very large circuit board, bigger than all the others, and mounted with lots of integrated circuits (black boxes with many legs), both small and large. This is the computer's *motherboard*, which contains all of your PC's most vital components. At the heart of the motherboard, you should find a flat, square chip, about 2cm square: this is the central processor unit (CPU), your computer's brain – the bit you call the Pentium, or 486, etc.

The motherboard contains several long sockets, which may or may not be filled with long chips. These sockets (grouped together in pairs known as *banks*) hold your computer's memory, its RAM. Before going out and buying any RAM modules, you should ensure that your motherboard has enough free banks.

Ports, expansion slots and buses

By now, you should have identified some of your PC's expansion cards. These typically have two major connection points with other components: an external socket, or *port*, which finds its outlet at the back of your computer; and an internal plug, which connects to your motherboard. Notice how the number of external sockets on the back of your computer corresponds to the number and position of internal sockets on your motherboard.

Most of these expansion cards should be near to each other, and are probably roughly the same size as each other. Next to the existing expansion slots, there may be some empty slot areas which are covered with metal plates, in order to keep out dust. For every blanked-out expansion slot, there should be a corresponding slot on your motherboard. These metal plates are held in place by a screw; to install an expansion card, you need to remove the screw, take out the plate, and then use the screw to fix the new card's port to the PC's external casing.

To a certain extent, then, installing a new card in your computer is just a matter of removing the protective metal plate from an opening on the back of your computer, and inserting the card into the motherboard's expansion slot that corresponds to that opening. However, it is not quite as simple as this, for there are several different types of expansion slots, and the cards that you plug into them must be compatible with the slot type.

A PC's expansion slots are connected to the CPU by means of a group of wires known as a *bus*. The different types of bus (including ISA, EISA, VESA, PCI and USB) each have different ways of carrying their data, and use different connectors to interface with the PC's components. The first bus type was the ISA (it stands for "*Industry Standard Architecture*") which transmitted data eight bits at a time. Later on, a 16-bit version of the ISA bus was developed, which transmitted data at twice the speed. The next improvement on this was the EISA (*Extended Industry Standard Architecture*), which was a 32-bit card.

The 16-bit ISA and the 32-bit EISA sockets are backwards compatible, which means that you can place an 8-bit ISA card into any ISA or EISA socket, and a 16-bit ISA card into an EISA socket – but you can't use a high-specification card in a lower-specification socket.

As a result of the increased power and complexity of the graphics used by modern PCs, additional "local" bus types have been developed which allow graphics cards to communicate directly with the CPU, bypassing the ISA or EISA bus. The first of these was the VESA (*Video Electronics Standards Association*), which has now been superseded by the faster PCI (*Peripheral Component Interconnect*).

The USB (*Universal Serial Bus*) is another innovation, not designed for the improvement of graphics, but to allow serial devices like joysticks or mice to transmit data faster.

Memory

When you buy extra memory for your computer, it will come in the form of a number of microchips stuck to a board, known as a SIMM, or *Single In-line Memory Module*. Along one edge, it will have a row of perhaps 72 metal connector tabs: these are what you should insert into the memory expansion slot on your computer's motherboard. One end of the card is usually cut away, making it asymmetrical, so that it is impossible for you to insert the card the wrong way round.

Before you buy some SIMM memory, you need to know how much you require. You might be able to determine this from the memory specifications required by your various pieces of software – some require at least 32Mb. Now find out how much memory you already have. To do this, click with your right mouse button on the My Computer icon on your Windows desktop. Now select *Properties* from the pop-up context menu, and choose the *Performance* tab. Next to the heading *Memory* you should see something like '16.0 MB of RAM', and next to *System Resources* perhaps '90% free'. If the memory specified here is less than suggested by your software's manufacturers, or if your system resources (the amount of memory currently available for any new application you might want to open) seem to be lacking, you should probably work out how much extra memory you need.

Unfortunately, buying extra memory is often not quite as simple as going down to your local computer shop and asking for the required number of megabytes. What you need to buy depends on the design of your PC, and on the amount of extra memory you want. For instance, let us say you need an extra 16Mb. You are likely to need two separate 8Mb SIMMs, each fitting into its own socket. (Each pair of SIMM sockets is known as a *memory bank*.) To find out what denominations you need to buy your memory in, you should contact the manufacturer of your PC, explaining what model it is and roughly how much extra memory you think you need. They should then be able to suggest exactly what SIMMs you need and where you can get them. If your expansion sockets are already full up, don't despair: you may be able to remove some low-capacity SIMMs and replace them with higher-capacity ones.

Memory modules are very easily damaged by static electricity, so when handling them you should take precautions to ensure that your body has not accumulated a dangerous amount of static from your environment: this is particularly likely if you have nylon carpets. This is not as much of a problem as it sounds, and simply requires that you are careful about what you touch while fitting memory chips. One of the easiest precautions you can take is to use a wooden work surface, which will discharge any static: when working with computer memory modules at least, touching wood is lucky! You should also try to balance out the static electricity between yourself, your computer and the new memory module by making sure that, throughout the process, you are touching both the SIMM and a metal surface of the computer. This way, there will be no dangerous surges of static between the different elements as differently-charged components come into contact with each other.

Once you have earthed yourself, locate the spare slot where you intend to insert the SIMM. At both ends of the slot you should be able to see a plastic support, which keeps the SIMM in place, and allows you to guide the SIMM into the right position in its slot. These plastic supports can be fragile, and you should be very careful not to break them. If you do break one, that slot may be rendered incapable of holding a SIMM. Often, it may not be possible to repair the slot, meaning that you may have to replace your whole motherboard (very expensive!) if you want to add to your PC's memory. Initially, you should insert the SIMM at an angle, and then, once it is in line, straighten it up vertically as you push it home into its slot.

Once you have inserted your SIMMs, close the case back up, reconnect all the cables, and turn your computer on as normal. You should find, in the initial DOS-like screen which tests your PC's memory, that the extra memory provided by your new SIMMs is recognised automatically. It's usually as simple as that – you need do nothing more. However, if you have an old computer which doesn't automatically recognise new memory, you may need to enter your CMOS setup program and alter your memory settings manually. (The key combination you must use to do this should be displayed on the opening screen.)

CPU

This is the most drastic act of upgrading you could perform on your computer, being akin to a brain transplant. Do not be too hasty to replace your CPU (*Central Processor Unit*): if you find your PC increasingly overburdened with large and complex programs, taking ages to do even the simplest task, your initial, logical reaction might be to give it a new brain. It might, however, benefit much more (and much more cheaply) from being given a little extra RAM. For example, a 100MHz Pentium with 16Mb of RAM will run most applications notably faster than a 133MHz Pentium with 8Mb of RAM. See the *Memory* section above first, then come back if that doesn't do the trick.

Whether or not it is worth your while buying a new CPU will depend on the type of motherboard you already have, and the compatibility of all your peripheral components with the CPU you propose to buy. (The *motherboard*, incidentally, is the large printed circuit board you will find when you open up your computer, containing all of the major components of your computer, including the CPU and the memory.) Some CPU chips, particularly the old 386SX processors, are not removable from your motherboard – they are soldered directly on to it – and so if you want to upgrade your processor you'll need to change the whole motherboard. However, there can be very few reasons for someone to want to upgrade such an old computer today: the implied expense of the procedure, with regard to the additional changes you would have to make to other components, would make it probably cheaper, and certainly more cost-effective, for you to throw away your old computer (or give it to charity) and start over with a shiny new Pentium.

On the other hand, if you have a fairly high-spec 486DX processor, or a low-end Pentium, a faster Pentium chip (e.g., 200MHz) could be just the thing you need to speed up your PC's performance, if you already have all the RAM you need. As with memory upgrades, you should consult your computer's manufacturer as to whether a CPU upgrade is advisable. If it is, the process should be fairly simple. The chip is a flat, square object, with 'legs' (connector pins) on all four sides. These legs slot into a matching set of sockets soldered to the motherboard. All you should have to do is prise the old

CPU off the socket unit, then slot the new one into place. Your manufacturer will tell you if you need to change anything else.

Hard drive

Only four or five years ago, you might have bought a computer with a 40-Megabyte hard drive (having the storage capacity of roughly 28 floppy disks); nowadays, it would be difficult for you to find a computer dealer trying to sell PCs with anything less than 1 Gigabyte (1,000 Megabytes, or 694 floppies).

When you come to buy a new hard drive, you need not only the drive but also a matching controller (another piece of hardware), which interfaces between the CPU and the drive, allowing the correct information to be retrieved from the correct place as and when it is needed. You cannot use just any old controller: it must be one that was designed to be used with your specific hard drive. You may also find, if upgrading your CPU, that the new CPU will not work with your old hard-drive controller, in which case you will have to see if a controller is available that can translate between the two.

If you have the available drive bays, and if you already have a functional hard drive that you would like to leave where it is, then you can always simply buy a second hard drive. These will not integrate seamlessly as a new, unified storage device, but will be treated by your computer as two separate media. If your original hard drive has the letter C: assigned to it, and if you don't already have a CD-ROM drive fitted, the new one would probably be named D: – and you could transfer information between the two just as you would between a hard drive and a floppy drive.

In choosing a hard drive, the major factor you are likely to consider after its storage capacity is the access time, which is measured in milliseconds. This is not the time that it takes to retrieve a piece of data from the hard drive (which would depend on the length of the data being retrieved), but the time taken by the drive's reading head to locate the place on the disk that it is looking for, and to begin accessing it. As you might expect, this figure depends jointly on the physical drive mechanism and on the efficiency of the controller hardware.

The possible difficulties involved in fitting a new hard drive and an appropriate hard drive controller may mean that it would probably be a simpler and better option for many people to fit a *Jaz* drive instead. These can be external drives which use special removable disks that have a capacity of 1 Gigabyte. It is possible simply to connect a Jaz drive to your PC's parallel port (the one that you would normally plug a printer into), but the relative sluggishness of this port would make disk access time noticeably slower than that of a hard drive. A much better option would be to connect a Jaz drive via a SCSI port. In order to do this, you need to have installed a SCSI adapter.

SCSI (*Small Computer Systems Interface*) is a type of data bus designed especially to interface high-speed hardware devices with a PC; it's much faster than a parallel or serial interface. A SCSI adapter fits into one of your PC's expansion slots (just like a sound card or internal modem) and allows you to connect up to seven internal or external SCSI devices to your PC. Each SCSI device has an input and an output socket. The first device you fit communicates directly with the SCSI adapter via its input socket; any subsequent devices tap into the SCSI bus by connecting their input socket to the output socket of another SCSI device. Thus, a chain of SCSI devices is formed: a special terminator is fitted to the output socket of the last member of the chain.

The beauty of connecting a Jaz drive to your computer using SCSI is that the speed of the interface allows you to work from the Jaz drive just as if you were using a hard drive. If your hard drive is running out of space, you can then store any new data on your Jaz drive instead; you could even install new applications onto the Jaz drive. This gives you a virtually limitless amount of storage space for all your software: when you eventually use up the Gigabyte of storage space on a Jaz disk, you can simply buy another one, for a fraction of the cost of buying a new hard drive.

Video card and monitor

Before you decide to upgrade your video card, consider whether or not you can improve your display simply by making some changes to the software display settings governed by Windows. For instance, it may be that you are using inferior display driver software. Choose *Settings>Control Panel* from the Start menu, double-click on the *Display* icon, and select the *Settings* tab. By clicking on the *Change Display Type* button, you can select from all the available drivers that are compatible with your graphics card and monitor. The Settings tab also allows you to change the number of colours that your PC is capable of displaying. The default Windows setting is "256 Color", but you can let Windows display more colours by choosing "High Color" or "True Color" from the drop-down menu. However, there is always a trade-off between the number of colours a graphics card can display, and the speed at which it displays those colours.

If you notice that videos and animations are displaying slower than normal when using an enhanced colour display, you may be better off switching back to 256 colours.

If you have decided that you need to replace the video card, however, open up your PC's case. Locating the slot into which you should insert your new video card is easy, since you must already have a lower-specification video card installed: it's the card that extends back from the port where you plug in your monitor's signal cable. Holding the edges of your old card, gently remove it, then insert the new one in its place. Replace your PC's case, and reconnect its cables. Now turn on your computer. If you see the normal automatic diagnosis screen which counts your PC's memory, you have installed your video card correctly. If, on the other hand, the screen is blank, you have a problem – check that you have reconnected your monitor cables correctly. If it still doesn't work, and if the video card is sitting snugly in its socket, you could have a device conflict. You might then have to remove one or more of the other expansion cards in order to get your video card to work; once you have done this, and you have a display, it may be possible to alter the allocation of your PC's resources in order to get all of your cards working.

If the problem with your display is not that it displays images too slowly or with too few colours, but that the image you see is too small, or it flickers, the chances are that you need a new monitor, not a new graphics card. You may pay a little more for a 15-inch monitor than for a 14-inch one, but the apparent improvement in the size and quality of the image is usually well worth the extra expense.

A flickering screen is usually caused by a low refresh rate. Most modern monitors display at a rate of at least 70 Hz – that is, the screen refreshes itself at least 70 times per second. A refresh rate lower than this may cause eye fatigue, especially if you regularly use your monitor for long periods.

The refresh rate aside, the quality of the picture produced by a monitor is defined using three variables: the number of colours it can support, the resolution of the image, and the sharpness of the image. The image's resolution is measured in the number of pixels (the dots used to make up the image) the screen can display; a typical resolution is 1024 horizontally, by 768 vertically, which you will see written as "1024x768". (If you see something like "1024x768x256", the third number refers to the number of colours the monitor can display.)

When we talk of the sharpness of a monitor's image, we are referring to the distance *between* the pixels. A typical value is 0.28mm. The question of the resolution, sharpness and number of colours of a monitor's image should always be considered in tandem with the properties of the video card that is driving it: upgrading to a monitor capable of a resolution of 1024x768 pixels, when the video card is capable only of 800x600, will not result in a higher-resolution image. Having said that, most monitors you are likely to buy nowadays are not restricted to a single resolution, number of colours or refresh rate, but offer a range of possible combinations: they are known as "multi-synch": thus, they might be able to display a resolution of 1024x768 with a refresh rate of 70 Hz, or a resolution 640x400 at 84 Hz, etc. The monitor automatically determines the nature of the signal it is receiving from the video card, and sets itself accordingly.

To change a monitor, you don't need to open up the case of your PC; you simply unplug the old one, and plug in the new one.

Sound card

A sound card fits into an expansion slot just like a video card or internal modem, but differs from most other expansion cards in that it has several sockets which it uses to interface with the outside world. We'll look at these in a moment. First, install your sound card: open up the case of your computer, and remove the metal plate covering its port opening. Now, place the card in its slot and fix it to the PC's casing using the screw that held the metal plate. If you have a CD-ROM drive (you may be fitting one at the same time as your sound card), there may be a cable coming from it, labelled something like "CD audio". There should be a corresponding socket on the sound card where you can plug this in (refer to your manual): this allows you to play audio CDs through your sound card's speakers.

Replace the casing, then take a look at the ports of the new card. They should be labelled; if they are not, then a diagram illustrating the layout of the sound card's connections should be given in the user manual that came with the card. The most important socket is the one that goes to your speakers; if you don't connect any, then you'll only be able to hear your sound card's output via headphones. Next, there should be an external microphone socket: you can plug a normal microphone into this, in order to be able to record your own wave sounds on your PC (use the Windows Sound Recorder to do this – select *Programs>Accessories>Multimedia>Sound Recorder* from the Start menu). You will also find a "line in" socket, and a "line out" socket. "Line in" allows you to connect external audio sources to your sound card for use as input by your PC – e.g., the output from a hi-fi system or a tape recorder; "line out" allows you to send the output of your sound card to similar devices.

Finally, most sound cards have a MIDI connection socket. If you are involved in computer-generated music, you can use this to connect your PC to MIDI-compatible musical instruments. This will allow the PC to record the digital signals coming from such instruments, or to send signals to a number of instruments, controlling their performance. If you have no interest in MIDI music, you'll probably use this port anyway; it usually doubles a joystick port, to let you control computer games easily.

CD-ROM drive

Virtually any PC you buy today will come with a CD-ROM drive already installed. However, if it did not, and if your computer is capable of handling the kind of multimedia software that usually comes on CD-ROMs, you will open up a vast new range of software for your PC by installing a CD-ROM drive. Most drives are internal – i.e., they go inside your PC's casing. Usually, the only reason you might choose not to have an internal CD-ROM drive would be if you don't have an available slot for it. (If this is so, the installation of the drive will consist simply of plugging the external drive's connector into a socket on the back of the PC, and connecting an external power source.)

Look at the front of your PC's case: you should not see a seamless face of grey plastic, but a surface that is divided partly into a number of rectangular panels. Open up your computer's casing and look for your computer's hard drive (see the earlier topic *Opening up the case*). You should find that this resides behind one of those rectangular panels on the front of the case. Your floppy disk drive may use another slot parallel with this, or may be located elsewhere. Are there any slots free? If so, you should be able to fit your CD-ROM drive.

Remove the screws that hold the drive bay's protective panel in place, and slide the new drive into place. Use the screws to fix the drive securely onto the computer's casing and chassis. There should be a long, flat ribbon cable coming out of the back of the CD-ROM drive: this is used to carry data to and from the drive. Where you connect this depends on the type of drive it is: look at the user manual. It should tell you to connect the drive either to a SCSI adapter, or your sound card. There may also be an additional cable which you should connect to your sound card to allow sound from an audio CD to be played through your sound card's speakers. Once you have made all of the connections appropriate to your particular CD-ROM drive, replace the PC's casing.

Modem

Most upgradable PC elements, like sound cards, CD-ROM drives and hard drives, are installed within a computer's casing, if there is room for them: there is no reason why you should clutter up the surface of your desk unnecessarily. Modems, however, are an exception to this rule: while internal modems are very popular, people often fit an external modem even when they have an expansion slot which could accommodate it. This is because the front of an external modem is covered in flashing lights, which are often very useful in showing exactly what the modem is doing at a given time. These lights show when the modem is on-line (i.e., connected to the Internet via a telephone line), when it is transmitting and receiving data, etc. An internal modem does not have a panel of flashing lights on the front of the PC in which it lives; the only external evidence that there is a modem inside your PC's casing is the telephone cable coming out of the back of it. Of course, Windows can tell you what your internal modem is doing, but the feedback might not be as immediate as an external modem's lights

– especially when your Web browser causes your computer to hang, and you want to know whether you are still on-line, wasting your telephone bill. You have to decide which is more important to you – the space on your desk, or the need to know exactly what the modem is doing at any given time. Fitting an external modem is easy: you just connect its data cable to a serial port on the back of your PC, plug in an external power source, and plug its output cable into a telephone socket.

Fitting an internal modem is a little more complicated. First, you need to open up your PC's casing and find an empty serial expansion slot. Now remove the panel protecting the port space, and slot in the card. Replace the PC's case, and look at the output sockets provided by the card you have just installed. There should be two sockets, both of which look like the socket into which you plug your normal telephone. One of these is to be connected, via a cable, to your telephone socket; the other allows you to plug your telephone into the back of your computer so that you can use the telephone from the same desk as the computer, without having to install another telephone cable extension (this is optional).

Installing hardware via Windows

Once you have fitted a new piece of hardware into your PC, the installation process may be over if you are using Plug'n'Play devices. However, if Windows doesn't appear to have recognised the new hardware, you should try to let Windows acknowledge it via the Add New Hardware Wizard, or another device-specific Wizard. Select *Settings>Control Panel* from the Start menu. If you have just fitted a new modem, double-click on the *Modems* icon – this will start the Install New Modem Wizard. Otherwise, double-click on the *Add New Hardware* icon, and answer the questions that you are asked. If this doesn't work, you may have a device conflict.

Suppose, for instance, you install a new modem, only to find that it won't work because it tries to access the same area of your PC's memory that is already being used by your mouse. The Windows Hardware Conflict Troubleshooter will detect this conflict, and allow you to choose how to resolve it. For instance, you can change the area of memory that one of the hardware elements uses, or disable one of the components in order that the other may work freely. To start the Troubleshooter, select *Help* from the Start menu, choose the *Contents* tab, then choose *Troubleshooting>If you have a hardware conflict*, and answer the structured diagnostic questions.

Upgrading software

Installing or upgrading new software is generally even easier than fitting new hardware. You don't need to open up the PC's case and worry about dislodging cables or breaking expansion slots. Almost every Windows program you buy today will come with a tailor-made installation program, which automates the whole process of putting the software on your computer's hard drive. The only input required from you is usually to confirm that you do indeed want to install the software.

The packaging or instructions of a new piece of software usually explain very clearly which file you need to run to begin installing the application. However, Windows provides a utility which searches for the installation program and adds extra control to the installation process. To use this, select *Settings>Control Panel* from the Start menu, and double-click on the *Add/Remove Programs* icon. This starts the Install Program Wizard: insert the CD or floppy disk on which the software is provided, then click Next and follow the instructions given by the Wizard and the software's own installation program.

Often, you are given the opportunity to perform a customised installation by defining exactly which components of the software application are included. This is particularly useful in the case of a large software suite, such as Microsoft Office, which may contain elements that you are never likely to use. There is normally a button labelled "Custom", which you should click on to do this.

If, subsequently, you wish to add components to an existing application, you should select its name from the Add/Remove Programs Properties dialog box, insert the installation CD or floppy disk, then click on the Add/Remove button to start the program's customised installation program. You will then be allowed to select any of the application's components that you chose not to install before.

The Last Word

By reading this book you have progressed a great deal; from knowing very little about computers to becoming computer literate. You are now ready to venture even further into the PC world.

To buy your PC system, you will need to compare specific brands of hardware and software. This book has prepared you to understand the literature on these products, so that you can make a fair comparison.

This book will also help you to get started with using your PC. The Windows procedures covered in Section 4 will enable you to command your PC to do various tasks. Also, Section 5 on *The Internet* will help you to explain the fastest growing area in computing.

Once you are beyond this stage, there are several ways to progress further.

Books

There are thousands of different books that fall under the subject of computers. Most of these titles are on specific products such as *Word*, *Excel* or *CorelDRAW*. Although these software products come with basic user manuals, good computer books are much more readable than the manuals.

Most of the specialised computer books are quite expensive – however, Computer Step publish a very successful series of low-price books, called "in easy steps", covering essential features from most popular software applications. The current list of titles includes:

Access in easy steps
CompuServe UK in easy steps
CorelDraw in easy steps
Excel in easy steps
FrontPage in easy steps
HTML in easy steps
Internet Explorer in easy steps
Internet UK in easy steps
Microsoft Money UK in easy steps
Microsoft Office in easy steps
Microsoft Office 97 in easy steps
Microsoft Works in easy steps

Netscape Navigator in easy steps
PageMaker in easy steps
PagePlus in easy steps
PowerPoint in easy steps
Publisher in easy steps
Quicken UK in easy steps
Sage Instant Accounting in easy steps
Sage Sterling for Windows in easy steps
SmartSuite in easy steps
Windows 95 in easy steps
Word in easy steps
Word 97 in easy steps
WordPerfect in easy steps

Videos

Educational videos on general computer principles and on more specialised topics are also now available. These are sometimes as much as four times more expensive than the usual movie videos. These videos are really produced and priced to be used by businesses to train a number of staff rather than for a private individual. Computer videos are not sold through high-street stores but usually by mail directly by the publishers. Some computer dealers and leading computer booksellers also supply them. The development of DVD drives for PCs, which are faster than CD-ROM drives, and which can hold much more data, may mean that we can soon expect to see full-screen DVD tutorial videos on a PC's monitor, doing away with the need to look at a TV screen and operate a video recorder while a new user is trying to learn how to use a computer.

CD-ROMs

If you are already acquainted with computers, and have a little more cash to spare, you might consider learning from CD-ROM tutorial software. Multimedia technology now makes it possible to bring together some of the features of computer books and videos in a single resource. Many software products on CD-ROM come with an additional, interactive tutorial program, which introduces users to the basic features of the software by guiding them through a structured series of tasks using the program's interface. These CD-ROMs often include video clips, perhaps containing a welcome message from the program's creators and explaining some of the things you can use the software for.

You can now buy separate CD-ROMs – such as those produced by Microsoft Press – which provide a more thorough programme of tutorials, making use of more real-world applications of the software. One big advantage of having all these resources on one CD-ROM is that all the information you need is exactly where you need it, on your computer: you don't have to balance a manual on your knees while tapping away at the keyboard, and your video recorder and television don't have to be wrestled into the computer room. Also, whereas it might be possible to misinterpret the instructions from a book or video and then waste time trying to work out why the program isn't doing what you want it to, an interactive tutorial, like a human instructor, won't let you go far wrong: if you're not clicking on the button it expects you to click on, it will point out the correct one for you.

Having said this, if you haven't yet perfected the basics of using a PC – such as how to open an application, minimise a window, or play a CD-ROM, then a CD-ROM tutorial may not be suitable. One of the disadvantages of CD-ROM tutorials is that they use an unfamiliar medium to teach people about that medium. A book, meanwhile, provides a familiar helping-hand that allows new users to learn at precisely their own pace, and can be removed from the computer room for a few minutes' quiet reading when the user becomes sick of an insolent PC that obstinately refuses to behave.

Computer-based training (CBT)

Computer-based training, or CBT for short, is a term used to describe training packages that force you to use your PC to do the course. You interact with your PC to learn about the product and to do the exercises included in the course. The basic aim of CBT is to get the student to learn by practical experience. The good thing about using CBT is that you can progress at your own pace and nobody has to know how you are doing.

The main drawback of CBT is that it is more expensive than learning from books. CBT is, however, more effective and an interesting way of learning. It has become quite popular in businesses where a licence can be purchased from vendors to train a large number of staff.

Classroom courses

Classroom courses are offered by technical colleges, polytechnics and some universities. You can attend on full or part time basis, or take evening classes. The range of courses offered vary from basic computing to using leading software packages like *Microsoft Office*. The prices vary from college to college. They usually run during the school terms and throughout the summer period. Check with your local colleges on exact times and prices.

Classroom courses are also offered by private companies. These companies specialise in computer training. Again, their courses are aimed at businesses more than private individuals – indirectly, this means that they are expensive. Having said that, the quality of instructors used by most of these companies is high. To satisfy the business clients, these companies have to offer high standards.

User groups

Anyone who uses a computer is called a *computer user*, or simply a *user*. A user group is formed when a pool of people using the same product or service keep in contact with each other to share their ideas and experiences. User groups are formed to help and offer advice to the members with their computer or with using the software. Some of these are free to join but most of them charge a nominal fee.

Members of user groups keep in touch by regular meetings, newsletters, telephone helplines, and increasingly via the Internet.

Most of these user groups are independent from product vendors. However, they may maintain a close relationship. By joining user groups you can learn how to make the most of your computer or software. You can usually find answers to any problems you may be having with the product. You can even raise issues that bother you or make suggestions to the vendors on improving the product. Also, you usually get to know about any upgrades or any other changes earlier than you would otherwise.

Other ways to learn more about PCs are those already discussed in Section 3, *Shopping*. Read computer magazines, especially the news sections and product reviews. Visit computer exhibitions now and then to keep up with changes in the industry and to see any new products being launched.

Internet newsgroups

An increasingly popular alternative to joining computer user groups is to seek help from Internet newsgroups (see the appropriate topic in Section 5, *The Internet*). There are hundreds of newsgroups devoted to all manner of computer-related topics, particularly within the *comp.** hierarchy, but here are some that people new to using PCs are likely to find most useful:

> comp.sys.ibm.pc.*
> comp.sys.ibm.hardware.*
> comp.os.ms-windows.misc

Glossary

APPLICATION PROGRAMS

Programs that perform specific tasks relating directly to business functions such as accounting and word-processing. Examples include Quicken and Word.

ARCHIE

A utility that allows someone searching for a file from the Internet – especially from FTP resources – to get a list of sites holding that file. The user runs an Archie client program on their computer, logs on to an Archie server, then enters the name of the file they are looking for (or a part of it); they should receive a list of suitable sites which they can then access.

ASCII (pronounced 'Asky')

Stands for American Standards Code for Information Interchange. It is an agreed standard that specifies which numbers will represent which characters. Computers can only work with numeric digits so each character on your keyboard has to be converted to a number for processing.

BACKUP

A procedure to create an extra copy of a program or data.

It is usual to hold this spare (backup) copy on a different storage medium from the original. The backup copy can be used should the original data be corrupted or lost.

BINARY

A numbering system where a numeric digit can only be 0 or 1. The first digit from the right represents multiples of decimal 1, the second digit multiples of decimal 2, the third digit multiples of decimal 4, and so on. So a decimal 2 is a binary 10, and a decimal 3 is a binary 11. Computers count using the binary system.

BIOS

Stands for Basic Input Output System. BIOS is a piece of coding that is stored in the computer's ROM (read only memory). Its basic function is to control the interaction between the processor and other hardware such as disk drives, keyboard and monitor.

BIT

Derived from BInary digiT, the term bit is a binary number, 0 or 1. The computer internally can only recognise a 1 which represents an 'on' switch and a 0 which represents an 'off' switch electronically. Eight bits are grouped together to form a byte, to represent a character.

BOOT

To boot a computer means to start a computer. The process involves switching the computer on and having it load up the operating system such as Windows.

BUFFER

A temporary storage area within the system. A buffer holds data until the main device such as computer memory or printer is ready to process it.

BUG

An error in a computer program, usually present simply because the program has not been tested (and 'debugged') thoroughly enough before being released. A minor bug might, for instance, prevent the computer user from using some feature of a program that should really be available (e.g., hitting a certain key on the keyboard doesn't have the intended effect). At the other end of the scale, bugs can cause the loss of important data, or cause a computer to **hang** – to freeze in operation, requiring the user to **reboot**.

The phrase 'bug' was coined when an insect flew into a vulnerable part of an early computer and caused a component to overheat, shorting out a circuit.

BUS

An electronic circuit within the PC through which data passes to go from one component to another, e.g. from memory to the processor.

BYTE

A byte consists of eight bits and represents a character. Memory size and disk capacity are measured in number of bytes.

CACHE MEMORY

An expensive type of memory which can be read and written to at a much faster rate than the ordinary memory. Used to hold 'live' information that is used frequently by the processor. The overall benefit of memory caching is that programs work at much faster speeds.

CAD/CAM

Stands for computer aided design and computer aided manufacturing. CAD software allows draughtsmen to use computers to replace their drawing boards and tools for technical drawings and plans. CAM relates to use of computers to control robotic tools for manufacturing.

CD-ROM

Acronym for compact disc read-only memory. Just another medium for read-only-memory. A CD allows storage of masses of data – it offers storage capacity of up to 600 megabytes.

CHARACTER

A letter, numeral or a symbol that is on your keyboard or displayed on your screen.

CHIP

Short for microchip. A thin rectangular silicon wafer on which electronic circuits are built. It is boxed in a black or grey casing with metal contacts.

CLIENT

A program that you run on your computer in order to communicate over the Internet (or some other communications medium) with a remote **server** machine, often in order to download files from a site managed by the server – as in **FTP** transfers.

CLIPART

A computer-generated picture or drawing you can purchase and use within your own DTP work.

CLIPBOARD

An integral part of the Windows operating system, designed to allow data to be exchanged easily between different applications, or to be moved from one position to another within a single document. **OLE**-compatible applications may exchange data of different types, so for example a picture created in a drawing program can be placed in a word-processor document.

COMMS

Short for communications. The term is used to describe the process of transferring data from one computer to another via the use of modems and telephone lines. Not to be mixed up with networks, which involves connecting several computers (usually with cables) so that data may be shared.

CPU

An acronym for central processing unit, also referred to as microprocessor, or just processor. This is the component in a computer where all the work is done. It is the CPU that follows your commands and performs the specified tasks.

CURSOR

A flashing line on your screen. When you type on your keyboard, the characters will appear on your screen where the cursor is positioned. As you type, the cursor will advance automatically.

DATA

Information that is stored on disks or processed by programs. This may be name, address, amount and so on.

DATABASE

A collection of data stored in an orderly manner so that future retrieval for searching, sorting or printing is easily achieved. Also used to refer to software that provides facilities to do this. The proper name for this type of software is a database management system (DBMS).

DEFAULT

When there is more than one option or setting available, the computer will be programmed to select one, usually the most common one, as the default. If you do not specify any preference, the computer will take it that you wish to opt for the default setting or option and continue processing accordingly.

DEVICE DRIVER

A software program that will allow an operating system to work with specific hardware such as a printer or a scanner. You should get this program on floppy disk or CD-ROM when you purchase your hardware.

DIRECTORY
See **Folder**.

DISK
A medium used for permanent storage of computer based data and programs. Most disks have a form of magnetic coating on which data is recorded.

DISK CACHE
An area in computer's RAM (random access memory) which is used to hold a copy of frequently accessed data. It is quicker for the processor to access data from the memory rather than from the hard disk. Disk caching is a way of increasing processing speed by saving on this access time.

DISK CONTROLLER
A disk controller is a major component of a hard disk. It is a board that plugs into the motherboard. It controls the mechanism for accessing, reading and writing data to the hard disk.

DISK DRIVE
A disk drive is part of the system unit of a computer. It holds disks, reads data from disks and writes data on disks. A disk drive and a disk must be compatible in terms of physical size and capacity.

DOS

Short for Disk Operating System. DOS used to be the major operating system for the IBM PC and compatibles; Windows, for those who had it, was loaded subsequently, though DOS continued to run in the background. While Windows is a graphical, intuitive operating system, usually allowing the user to perform any action in one of a number of ways, DOS is wholly textual and much more linear. A large number of abstract commands must be memorised if the user is to take full advantage of the facilities available in DOS – making it a rather daunting environment for the newcomer to computers. The arrival of Windows 95, which did not require DOS running in the background, has largely done away with the need for DOS.

DOWNLOAD

To copy a file from another, remote computer to your own. When you get any file from the Internet, e.g. from an FTP or Web site, you are downloading it. Compare **upload**.

DPI

An acronym for dots per inch. DPI is used to measure resolution of output from scanners and laser printers.

DRIVER

The software that tells a computer how to operate a peripheral, such as a printer. When you buy a new printer, for instance, it will usually come with a floppy disk containing its driver software, which you should install before trying to operate the printer. The Windows CD-ROM contains lots of driver software for all types of devices.

DTP

Short for Desktop Publishing and means using a computer to combine text and graphics on a page to produce magazines, newsletters, books etc. Replaces time-consuming traditional methods of manually cutting and pasting text/graphics. Also used to refer to software that provides facilities to achieve this, such as PageMaker, QuarkXpress, Ventura and PagePlus.

DVD-ROM

A type of high-capacity data-storage disk; the acronym DVD is variously explained as standing for "*Digital Video Disk*" or "*Digital Versatile Disk*". The DVD-ROM disk can hold at least six times the amount of information held by a CD-ROM, making it ideal for storing not only huge amounts of computer data, but also full-length, full-screen, TV-quality movies. A DVD-ROM disk looks exactly the same as a CD-ROM disk, but uses three basic methods to squeeze on more data: (1) the pits on the surface of the disc used to store the data are squashed more tightly together; (2) the disks are double-sided, not single-sided like the CD-ROM; (3) each side of the disk has several transparent layers of data, built on top of each other – the laser used to read the disk adjusts its focus depending on which layer it wants to read.

EDUTAINMENT

A type of software using media traditionally associated with entertainment (such as sound, video, brightly-coloured computer graphics, etc.) to enhance the learning process in an educational environment. For example, an encyclopedia, traditionally confined to using text and pictures within the pages of a book, can offer much more when developed for multimedia-capable computers. While a picture is worth a thousand words, a suitable animation is often worth a thousand pictures.

E-MAIL

A system which allows sending and receiving of messages between users of the Internet, or another type of network.

EMOTICONS

Short sequences of **ASCII** characters which are meant to

resemble human faces in various states of emotion. They are popular on the Internet, where the main means of self-expression is still textual; a well-judged emoticon might clarify that a sentence intended as a friendly joke is not in fact a personal attack. You normally have to twist your head round by 90° to see an emoticon's graphical effect. The most common are smiling :-) and unhappy :-(

EMULATION
A way of programming a computer or software to believe and behave as if it were another.

EXPANSION CARD/SLOT
A circuit board that fits into an expansion slot on the motherboard inside the computer. Just as the name implies, it allows you to add extra features such as more memory or to connect a modem to the PC.

FAQ
Frequently Asked Questions. As the Internet's population rapidly grows, an increasing number of people find themselves in a communications environment different from any other they have experienced, and where there already exist a confusing, slightly alien set of conventions and rules of etiquette. These new arrivals understandably

have a lot of questions to ask others about the places they decide to visit – such as Web sites or Usenet newsgroups. Old hands may eventually tire of answering the same questions, and so FAQ files are placed where new visitors might easily find them. These files contain lists of answers to the questions that are likely to be asked about a specific Internet site or activity. Before joining in at any social gathering place on the Internet, you should read the FAQ and spend some time **lurking**, in order to get a feeling for what sort of behaviour is and is not expected of you.

FILE
A collection of information held together under one entity. The information may be a program, customer data, a letter from a word-processor or a report from an accounting system.

FLAME
To send angry messages to someone via e-mail or Usenet, in response to a message that the sender has found offensive or inconsiderate. Flames are often answered in kind; when several flames and counter-flames have been exchanged, usually involving more than two people, the resulting phenomenon is known as a *flame war*.

FLOPPY DISK

A permanent form of storage medium that may be separated from the computer. The only type in popular use nowadays is the 3½ inch disk, though in the past 5¼ inch disks were used. 3½ inch disks are made with a stronger casing and, though dimensionally smaller, have a higher storage capacity.

FOLDER

A means of collecting files on a data storage medium (such as a **hard disk**) into sensible groups, making it easy to find the file you are looking for, and to handle groups of files of the same type. Folders can contain not only files, but also other sub-folders, making it possible to build up a tree-like organisational structure. Also known as *directories* – which is the terminology also commonly used when talking of other collections of files, such as FTP archives.

FONT

Means a particular type of typeface or a typestyle. E.g. Times New Roman, Script. The proper reference to a font should also include the point size and style (e.g. italics, bold). However, quite often the word font is used instead of typeface.

FORMAT

The process of preparing disks for use. Formatting a disk involves dividing it up and allocating areas for data storage.

FTP

File Transfer Protocol. Until recently, the standard method used by computers to exchange files over the Internet. An FTP site usually holds in its archive a vast amount of files available to the general public. These are stored in directories (or folders), just like those used to organise the files on your own hard drive. In order to download files by FTP, your computer needs to be running a **client** program, which you use to instruct the FTP site's **server** program about which files you want it to send you.

GIGABYTE

A gigabyte is equal to a thousand million bytes (to be exact 1,073,741,824 bytes), which is equal to one million kilobytes or a thousand megabytes.

GOPHER

A utility allowing users to search by topic for files located on the Internet. This differs from Archie, which requires the name of the file that is being searched for. One Gopher server is likely to differ from another in terms of the sites to which it provides access, and the way it catalogues these resources. Gopher was the precursor of the World-Wide Web, which today largely supersedes it. However, you might find a need to visit 'Gopherspace' if you are searching for the kind of file that might be hard to find on the multimedia-geared Web – e.g., simple text files.

GRAPHICS

Refers to pictures and drawings including lines, circles, squares or any other shapes produced using a computer. The term is also used to refer to software that allows you to draw and manipulate these objects.

Computer graphics can be divided into two types: *bitmap graphics*, which represent an image as a grid of dots, each assigned a value according to the colour found there; and *vector-based graphics*, which represent the different elements of a comparatively simple image using mathematical values which remain constant no matter how much the image is expanded or contracted.

GUI (pronounced 'gooey')

Short for graphical user interface. A friendly interface between the computer and the user; an alternative to a command-based interface like DOS. GUI usually provides option menus and icons (symbols) to make it easier to operate the computer. The most popular GUI product for the PC today is Windows by Microsoft.

HACKER

A person who is obsessed with computers. Often used to refer to a person who accesses and manipulates other people's computers without obtaining authority.

HANG

When a computer 'freezes' whilst performing an operation, often as the result of a **bug** in a program, or a conflict of different hardware devices. Often the only option available is to **reboot**.

HARD DISK

A fixed disk usually installed inside the computer for the purpose of storage. It has far higher capacity and it is much more efficient to use than a floppy disk. For any serious work you must have a hard disk on your system; all modern PCs come with one built-in.

HARDWARE

The physical, tangible parts of a computer and its peripherals. A CD-ROM drive is hardware, as is the CD-ROM disk it reads; the information contained on the CD-ROM disk is **software**.

HOST

In computer communications, a remote computer running **server** software which permits users to access data held in its storage facilities, or else connect to some other computer or network via a connection to which they would not otherwise have access.

HTML

HyperText Markup Language. The native language of the World-Wide Web, allowing Web pages to be created easily by adding special "tags" to normal text, to enhance it, and to add extra media such as pictures, sounds and videos. For example, to put a piece of Web-page text in italics, you would enclose it within <I>these special italic tags</I>.

Hz

An abbreviation for Hertz, which is a unit of frequency meaning "one cycle per second". Hertz – more particularly Megahertz (1 million Hertz) – are used to define the speed at which many of the components of a PC operate. For example, a 200 Megahertz (usually abbreviated to MHz) Pentium processor performs 200 million operations every second.

ICON

A visual picture or a symbol used to represent programs or documents in a GUI environment.

INTEGRATED SOFTWARE

Integrated software is a combination of applications packaged together and treated as one product. It usually consists of a word-processor, database, spreadsheet and some utility programs. An example of an integrated package is Works by Microsoft.

INTERLACED/NON-INTERLACED MONITORS

Super VGA monitors which offer very high resolution may be interlaced or non-interlaced. The difference between the two is in the way they update screens. Screens are updated by electron beams defining each dot on a screen in turn. This is usually done in one go (referred to as one scan). However, with high resolution Super VGA screens, the number of dots to be updated is extremely high, making it expensive to update all the dots in one scan. To make screens more economical, interlaced screens are designed to update every other line in the first scan and the rest in the next scan. Unfortunately, this causes the screens to flicker. Non-interlaced screens update the whole screen in one scan and you will not have the problem of flickers. However, these are more expensive.

INTERNET
A global network used by computers to communicate with each other. It was born in the United States in the Cold War years, when the military deemed it necessary to have some means of communication that would not be put out of action in the event of a nuclear attack. Its strength lay in its design, a complex, non-linear tangle of connections between different computers: if some connections were attacked and severed, any base should still be able to communicate with any other by using alternative lines. The Internet now spans the globe, and is increasingly becoming a medium for personal and commercial communication, but the principle of decentralisation upon which it was created continues to be expressed in an anarchic, ungoverned atmosphere.

INTERNET RELAY CHAT (IRC)
The Internet version of telephone chat-lines or CB radio. Like **Usenet**, IRC is organised into channels, according to topic of interest; unlike Usenet, IRC is an immediate experience, allowing communication in 'real time'. Anyone can create a channel immediately, if they feel that an IRC venue of a certain type is either missing or

overcrowded, and if they expect that anyone else will visit it. This person then becomes the operator of the channel, with the privilege of inviting others and rejecting those who decide to visit. A simple textual interface is used, by which people type messages in at their keyboard, and see them displayed on the screen underneath the messages sent previously by everyone else on that channel. A conversation between many people can thus spring up, just as it might in any crowded room.

INTRANET

A network developed specifically for a company or other organisation, which uses the Internet as a medium for allowing members of that organisation to communicate effectively, where normal Internet facilities would not be adequate. For example, if a chain of high-street shops needs to allow its branches to exchange sales and stock data with each other, the best way of doing this using normal Internet means would be via e-mail. However, this is not an immediate form of communication: the data is not displayed until someone decides to read it. Alternatively, the company could develop an Intranet, to which all branches were permanently connected, which would make any data submitted by any branch instantaneously available to all other branches.

ISDN

Integrated Services Digital Networks. A digital communications network intended to replace the current system of telephone lines, which will still allow normal voice communication, but which also offers the increased bandwidth that is necessary for high-speed digital communication. When ISDN has become established, computers will be able to exchange data with each other directly at a very high rate, without the need for **modems** to convert their digital signals into the electrical audio signals required by normal telephone lines.

JAVA

A programming environment developed for use on the Internet, which enables small programs to be contained in World-Wide Web pages, regardless of the type of computer that is being used to view them. Thus, a Web page containing an applet could be accessed just as effectively by a PC, a Mac, or a Network Computer (NC).

JPEG

A standard of compression used for still images – stands for *"Joint Photographics Experts Group"*. JPEG compression uses a special algorithm to determine areas of an image where a lot of detail is not needed; these areas are subtly filled in with a blank colour, in such a way that the eye is fooled into thinking it sees more detail than it is actually being shown. This innovative method of compression produces very small files, which are ideally suited for use on the Internet. A number of sequential JPEG images are combined with sound to form **MPEG** video files.

K
Short for Kilobytes. One Kilobyte may be referred to as just 1K.

KEYBOARD
The main hardware device for entering data in a computer. A computer keyboard looks very much like a typewriter keyboard, but has extra keys for specific computer functions.

KILOBYTE
One thousand bytes. To be precise, 1,024 bytes (or 2 to the power of 10).

LAN
An acronym for local area network. LAN computers are linked together with cables and they are usually under one roof.

LOAD
Moving a program or data into the computer's memory, usually from a disk.

LURKING
Observing the behaviour and conventions of people at a site on the Internet before joining in. If you are new to a Usenet newsgroup, for instance, you should spend some time reading the message threads before posting your own. This way, you will learn what sort of subject the newsgroup is concerned with, and get an understanding of the prevailing standards of behaviour, whether formal or casual, serious or light-hearted.

MACRO
One key or a command representing a sequence of keystrokes or commands. A number of frequently used keystrokes or commands may be defined and saved under one macro to avoid typing them again and again.

MAILING LIST
A method using e-mail of taking part in a discussion group on a particular subject of interest. A participant sends their name and e-mail address via e-mail to a mailing list server. These details are then added to a mailing list maintained by the server. Any contributions

to the discussion sent by e-mail to the server will then be redistributed automatically to everyone on that list.

MATHS COPROCESSOR
A microchip that can process calculations, especially those involving fractions, at a much faster rate than the processor. It is fitted inside the computer. Software such as spreadsheets can perform much faster if the computer has a maths coprocessor.

MEGABYTE
One million bytes. 1,048,576 bytes, to be precise. Also equal to one thousand Kilobytes.

MEMORY
A microchip that holds programs and data that are required by the processor. Unlike disks it only stores 'live' information.

MENU
A list of commands or options displayed on the screen, prompting the user to select one.

MHz
See **Hz**.

MICROPROCESSOR

Also known as a processor or a CPU (central processing unit). A microchip that actually performs all the specified tasks. It is installed on the motherboard inside the computer.

MIDI

Stands for musical instrument digital interface. An interface, including a port, for connecting musical instruments to the computer for composing music.

MODEM

Derived from MOdulator/DEModulator, it is a hardware device that is required for computers to be linked via telephone lines. A modem converts digital signals from computers to analogue signals required for transmission through the telephone system, and vice versa.

MONITOR

A synonym for computer screen, display or VDU. A monitor is the main device to see what you have typed and also for the computer to communicate to you.

MOTHERBOARD

Computer's main circuitry where the microprocessor and other chips are plugged.

MOUSE

An input device that is placed and moved around the desk to control cursor movements. It also has two buttons which may be used to select menu options and to manipulate text and objects on screen.

MPEG

The most popular standard of video compression – stands for "*Moving Picture Expert Group*". An MPEG file is simply an animated series of still **JPEG** images, with added sound.

MS-DOS

See **DOS**.

MULTITASKING

When a processor is performing more than one task at a time. Strictly speaking, the processor cannot really achieve this, but appears to be providing this service by executing a task (or a program) for a very short time and then switching to another task and so on. This technique is known as 'time-slicing' and it gives the impression that several programs are running simultaneously.

MULTIMEDIA

The art of using a computer for combining text, graphics, sound and video to present information.

NC

Network Computer. A computer developed for connection to the Internet, sacrificing many of the expensive and bulky components of a modern PC (such as a hard drive, powerful CPU and lots of RAM) for the sake of cheapness and portability. Instead of loading its software from a hard drive, a network computer downloads programs and data from the Internet.

The NC is the brainchild of four giants in the computing world: Oracle, Sun, IBM and Corel. The only two giants bigger than these – Microsoft and Intel – have partially jumped on the bandwagon with their own take on the NC, called the NetPC.

NETIQUETTE

The rules of etiquette that prevail on the Internet. Owing largely to the textual nature of many Internet facilities, the environment in which people find themselves is very different from that of 'real life'. Angry comments, which might be forgotten within seconds in a face-to-face situation, could be recorded indefinitely on someone's hard drive if made to a Usenet newsgroup. The conventions of Netiquette are intended to avoid unwanted hostilities, which might otherwise be caused by accident. As a way of conveying emotion in a text-based environment, some people use **emoticons**. Also, remember to avoid **shouting**.

NETWORK
A way of connecting computers so that they can share data, software programs as well as hardware such as printers.

NEWSGROUPS
See **Usenet**.

OLE (OBJECT LINKING AND EMBEDDING)
A Windows standard, supported by most applications, which allows data to be exchanged and shared by different programs. If a file is updated, any instances of it that have been embedded in other documents will not automatically be updated. On the other hand, all linked instances of the same file will be updated as the original file is changed. This is very handy for using the same data in different applications without having to enter it separately in each one. You decide whether to embed or link an object by choosing the appropriate option from the Edit menu.

ONLINE
Programs/information which can be accessed and made

available from the computer immediately, without having to load them in from external storage media.

OPERATING SYSTEM

An operating system consists of a suite of programs that interface between the user, applications programs and the processor. It translates commands into machine language that the computer understands. It also controls the hardware and software. The most common operating system for PCs is **Windows**.

OS/2

Stands for Operating System/2. An operating system for the PC and PS/2 intended by IBM to succeed DOS and Windows.

PACKET

A unit of **data** of a certain size, as used in communication either between different computers, or between different components of the same computer. For example, all data sent over the Internet is split up into packets of 256 **bytes**. These are then sent by whichever route is the most convenient at the split-second they need to be transmitted, and then reassembled in their correct order at the other end. Packets break the data down into manageable units, and also help to protect against the large-scale corruption of transmitted data: if one packet is not sent successfully, then only that packet need be sent again – not the whole body of data.

PARALLEL PORT

A port is a socket at the back of a computer where another device can be plugged into for exchanging information. A parallel port sends data a byte at a time and therefore it is faster than a serial port. It is usually used for connecting a printer and it is also known as a Centronics port.

PC

An acronym for 'Personal Computer'. Used to refer to all microprocessors, but since IBM introduced the IBM PC, it is used to mean the IBM PC and compatibles.

PERIPHERAL

Any device that is connected to the main computer, such as a printer or a modem.

PING

Packet Internet Groper. A small utility that you can use to help test whether or not your **Winsock** software is working properly. It simply sends **packets** of data to an Internet site of your choosing, and waits to see if it gets a signal back from the site to tell it that the data was in fact received. If no such signal is received, you probably need to reconfigure your Winsock.

PIXEL
A PICture ELement, or a dot on the computer screen. A pixel is the smallest element a screen can be divided into. The number of pixels a screen can generate determines the resolution – the higher the number of pixels the sharper the image.

PLUG 'N' PLAY
A concept employed by the Windows operating system which aims to simplify the addition of peripherals to a computer system. Before Plug 'n' Play, anyone wanting to connect a new peripheral (such as a modem) to their PC had to run a complicated setup program which established the properties of the new component with respect to the existing ones, in order to avoid hardware conflicts (e.g., two pieces of hardware trying to use the same part of the computer's memory). A device supporting Plug 'n' Play technology automatically informs Windows of its specifications, and Windows manages the sharing of computer resources more or less automatically, without requiring the intervention of the user.

PORTABLES

Computers that are designed to be carried around. Portables should be light and compact enough to be moved easily. Many of the models work on batteries so they can be used whilst on the move.

POSTSCRIPT

A language that instructs a laser printer what to print. It is referred to as a page description language because it defines the page to be printed rather than giving a set of instructions on what to print. Postscript laser printers are printers that can understand this language. For professional DTP work you will need a Postscript printer.

PRINTER

A hardware device that a computer needs to produce information on paper.

PROCESSOR

See **CPU**.

PROGRAM

A set of coded instructions for the computer to perform a specific task. There are two types of programs: system programs which include operating systems, and application programs such as word-processors and spreadsheets.

PUBLIC DOMAIN SOFTWARE

Software that the author has decided to distribute freely rather than selling it for a price. This means you should neither pay for it nor sell it. You can copy it and use it as you like.

RAM

An acronym for Random Access Memory. Storage memory inside the computer that may be written to and updated by the processor. RAM only holds 'live' data, which means that any updates must be saved on a hard or floppy disk before leaving the application or switching off the computer.

REAL TIME CLOCK

A battery powered clock inside the computer that maintains the time and date, even when the computer is switched off.

REBOOT

To restart the operating system of your computer – often required after a program has been caused to **hang** as the result of a bug or an unforeseen hardware conflict. In Windows, pressing the keys *Ctrl*, *Alt* and *Delete* should summon a dialog box that allows you to close down a specific application that has stopped responding, or else to reboot your PC. If this doesn't work, you may have to press the reset button on your computer's case, effectively turning the computer off and on again. When you install a new piece of hardware, or make important changes to your system settings, you are often required to reboot your computer before the changes can take effect. You can reboot Windows at any time by clicking on *Shut Down...* from the *Start* menu, and then selecting the appropriate menu option.

RECYCLE BIN

A feature of Windows which acts as a safeguard against the accidental deletion of files. When a file is 'deleted' using Windows Explorer or My Computer, it is not actually removed from the computer system, but simply sent to the Recycle Bin – and will remain there until you empty the bin as part of your Windows 'housekeeping' duties. If you change your mind, it is a simple matter to restore a file to its original place.

RESOLUTION

This determines how well defined text/graphics appear from a computer screen, printer or even from a scanner. The higher the number of dots (or pixels) representing output from these devices, the higher the resolution.

ROM

An acronym for Read Only Memory. ROM is storage memory inside the computer that cannot be amended or erased by the processor. ROM is used to hold static information necessary for the computer such as the Basic Input Output System (BIOS).

SCANNER

A hardware device that can read in visual images from paper and convert them into data files that can be manipulated by the computer. Hand-held scanners (which are ideal for small, low-resolution images) are available very cheaply, but for high-quality images an expensive flatbed scanner should be used.

SCSI

Small Computer System Interface. A type of data **bus** designed to interface high-speed hardware devices with a PC – much faster than a parallel or serial interface. Several components, internal or external, can be linked to a SCSI interface, forming a chain.

SERIAL PORT

A port is a socket at the back of a computer where another device can be plugged in for exchanging information. Unlike the parallel port, a serial port transmits data one bit at a time. Used mainly for connecting a mouse or modem to a PC.

SERVER

A program running on a computer (often referred to as the 'host') at a remote site, used to manage the site's archive of files and allow others to access that archive (usually via the Internet). In order to communicate with a server, your computer needs a matching **client** program.

SERVICE PROVIDER

A commercial organisation providing Internet access to those with no permanent Internet connection. Service providers are directly and permanently connected to the Internet, and allow their clients to use a modem to achieve a temporary 'dial-up' connection via the telephone line. For this privilege they charge a fee, usually monthly, which normally grants the user unlimited access to the Internet. In the UK, the telephone bill which must additionally be paid is invariably more expensive than the service provider's fee.

SHAREWARE PROGRAMS

Shareware is really a way of marketing computer software. Shareware programs are distributed freely like public domain software. However, authors request a nominal fee if you decide to continue using the software. When you register by paying your fee you will receive proper manuals and future updates.

SHOUTING

The practice of typing with the Caps Lock button permanently on, either because it eliminates the need to hit the Shift button at the beginning of sentences, or in the mistaken belief that it makes text clearer. New users of e-mail and Usenet Newsgroups are often reprimanded by old hands for shouting, because IN FACT IT MAKES TEXT VERY DIFFICULT TO READ.

SIMM

Single In-line Memory Module. A card containing a number of microchips that provide a PC with its **RAM**. To upgrade your PC's RAM, you must add a pair of SIMMs: they slot into a pair of sockets known as a *memory bank*.

SOFTWARE

Software consists of data and coded instructions (programs) for the computer. Software is held on hardware such as disks and memory.

SOUND CARD

A hardware device that is inserted into a computer in order to allow it to play high-quality music and sound effects, and to allow sounds to be recorded digitally by the computer. An essential part of any modern multimedia system, most sound cards offer MIDI capability, allowing data to be exchanged with compatible musical instruments in terms of musical notes, not raw sounds. Additionally, many new sound cards offer sophisticated wave-table sound synthesis, derived from analysis of the sounds of real musical instruments.

SPREADSHEET

A spreadsheet is a method of performing elaborate calculations using rows and columns. A computer based spreadsheet allows you to assign value, text or formula to each element on the spreadsheet (known as a 'cell'). Once a formula is assigned to a cell, its value will be automatically calculated. A computer can also work out the effect of a change almost instantly. This makes it very useful for 'what if?...' analysis which would be very tedious and time-consuming to work out manually. Software packages that offer these facilities are also known as spreadsheets. Examples include Lotus 1-2-3 and Excel.

SURGE PROTECTOR

A peripheral device that protects the computer from power surges from the outlet where the PC is plugged in.

SVGA

Super Video Graphics Array is a display standard for PC monitors. Super VGA offers a screen resolution of up to 1280 x 1024 pixels. At high resolutions like this, the number of colours you can display depends on your video RAM; 4MB will give you up to 16,000,000 colours.

TCP/IP

Transmission Control Protocol/Internet Protocol. The standards of data communication used to allow different computers (from different sub-networks) on the Internet to talk to each other using a common language. Your computer uses a piece of software called a **Winsock** to achieve TCP/IP communication.

TELNET

A text-based means of operating remote computers over the Internet, using command-line instructions. Telnet is a very old means of interfacing with other computers, and today there is usually a simpler, more graphically based way of doing what several years ago might have required you to learn a list of specific Telnet commands.

However, there are several activities for which you might still find Telnet useful, such as accessing university library catalogues.

TONER
Made of powder pigment, it is used by laser printers instead of ink to print an image.

TRACK BALL
An input device used instead of a mouse. It looks like an upside-down mouse, with the ball at the top. Instead of moving the whole device for cursor movements you just rotate the ball.

TSR PROGRAMS
TSR is short for terminate and stay resident. TSR programs are designed to stay in the memory for easy access, when required. They can be activated by simply pressing a key or a combination of keys. Sometimes also referred to as memory resident programs.

TYPEFACE
A style for a set of characters. Sometimes called fonts. Examples include: Times Roman, Helvetica and Bookman.

UNIX

A very powerful operating system for personal computers developed by AT & T Bell Laboratories. It is also widely used in minis and mainframe computers. Unix is designed for multitasking and multiuser environments.

UPLOAD

To copy a file from your own computer to a remote computer. If you want to pass on a piece of **shareware** to other Internet users for instance, you might upload it to a **Usenet** newsgroup – from which other people could subsequently **download** it.

URL

Uniform Resource Locator. The Internet equivalent of a postal address. The URL of a World-Wide Web site, FTP site, etc., is entered into a text box in your Web browser or other client software. The software then follows the information given in the address to connect to the appropriate site. By studying a URL you can usually determine type of resource, the name of the organisation, the country in which it is located, and what sort of organisation it is. For example, *http:// www.barclays.co.uk* is the URL of the Web site used by Barclays bank, a commercial company, located in the UK.

USENET

A facility available on the Internet, allowing people to communicate by sending and responding to messages posted on what is effectively a global, electronic bulletin board. Usenet is divided into thousands of newsgroups, according to a hierarchy of subject topics, ranging from computing to cookery. Virtually any area of interest should be covered by at least one newsgroup. A message and its replies are organised into 'threads', from which readers may select any postings that seem interesting.

VIRTUAL REALITY (VR)

An artificial environment, generated by and existing in a computer. The types of media used to interact with this world determine how convincing a representation of an environment it actually is. At one end of the scale, you might see a virtually 3-dimensional world through a normal 2-dimensional computer monitor, and move through it by using your mouse to point where you want to go. On the other hand, a more convincing visual effect of being in a virtual world can be achieved by wearing goggles which use miniature screens to provide a separate image for each eye, thus creating a true 3-dimensional effect. A glove fitted with movement sensors may be worn, which is translated in the virtual world into a visible, moveable 'hand'. This can be used to manipulate the objects found there, just as one would with real, physical objects.

VIRUS
A piece of software that is designed to corrupt information on the computer. It is programmed to run automatically, copy itself and spread to other linked computers via floppies, local networks or the Internet.

VISUAL BASIC
A programming language that enables users to develop programs for the Windows operating system quickly and easily. The Visual Basic toolkit allows much of the programming to be done using a simple drag-and-drop interface. For example, to begin creating a dialog box of a certain size, you click on a button in the Visual Basic toolbar, and simply drag a rectangle to the desired size.

WINDOWS
A window is a generic term for a rectangular area on the computer screen which can be treated as an individual display that can hold information. Windows is also a GUI product by Microsoft which uses the concept of windows to allow running of more than one program simultaneously.

WINSOCK
The underlying communications software that needs to be running on your computer in order for an Internet connection to be achieved. A Winsock allows your computer to communicate with others on the Internet by using the standard **TCP/IP** communications protocol.

WORD PROCESSING
Using computers for producing letters and other documents. At its basic level, word processing supersedes the traditional typewriter, making it possible to edit text several times before finally printing it on paper. Today, most word processing packages offer a lot more than just the editing function: spell checking, macros, mail-merging and indexing are just a few examples.

WORLD-WIDE WEB (WWW)
A user-friendly, highly intuitive environment developed as a medium of communication for the **Internet**. While early means of exchanging information on the Internet used a mostly text-based medium, requiring the user to memorise many abstract commands in order to perform the simplest actions, the WWW is very visual, and is formed largely of 'pages' of text and pictures, much like those you would find in a magazine – though sound, video and virtual reality are playing an increasingly important

part in the growth of the Web, as a multimedia environment is created which is destined to be the major means of global communication and entertainment in the future.

One of the most exciting features of the Web is its utilisation of *hot-links*, tagged areas of a Web page, which allow the user to jump immediately to another related page simply by clicking on them with the mouse pointer. The process of using these hot-links to move from one Web page to the next, as you narrow down your search for a particular type of information – or discovering new areas of interest by following interesting, unanticipated links – is known as 'surfing the Web'.

WRITE PROTECT
A way of protecting data on floppy disks so that it does not get over-written or deleted. In one corner of a floppy disk you should find a small, square hole; a small, square piece of plastic may be slid over the hole in order to block it. If the plastic slider is in the retracted position, revealing the hole, then the disk is protected.

WYSIWYG (pronounced 'wizzy-wig')
Stands for 'What You See Is What You Get'. A facility in programs which can display text and graphics on your screen exactly as they will appear when printed on paper.

Index

Here are some endorsements received for earlier editions of this book:

"....the author has made sure that the entire book has been written in plain, simple language...Everything the beginner needs to know to get started is between these covers"

- Practical PC

"....an excellent little book for the novice user".

- PC Today

"....invaluable to get them (non-technical students) started"

- Secondary & Higher Education Journal

Also, recommended by the Booksellers Association and The Financial Times.